High Shelf

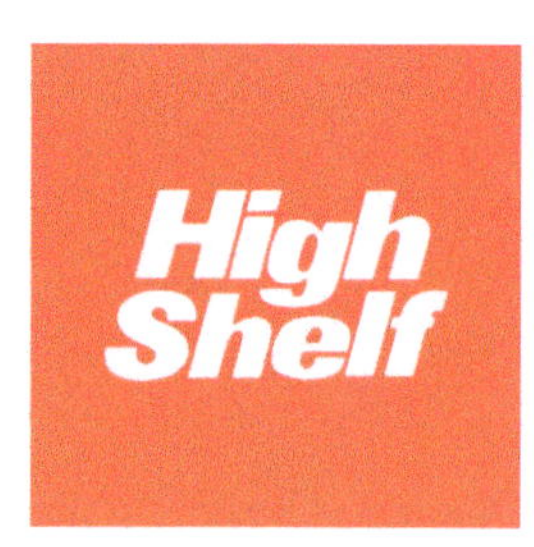

High Shelf XII, November 2019
Portland, Oregon.
Copyright 2019, High Shelf Press

ISBN: 978-1-7330279-9-1

Cover Image by *Meggan Joy*
Design and Layout by C. M. Tollefson
Edited by David Seung & C. M. Tollefson

High Shelf XII

November 2019

"(i)t has always been,
difficult;
searching, for
Love... "

Steven J. Wills

"...teach me to diminish.
Teach me to live
without wreckage."

Meimei Xu

Table Of Contents

The Storm that keeps me Home

Thomas Boos

At the bottom of the yard I see

The blue pine wrapped in its own limbs,

Throwing its head forwards and back.

Rolls of thunder chase after each other

In the deepening black of the sky.

My mother wraps herself in her shawl,

And looks older than I know her to be.

The window panes are set rattling

In the old frames, and the storm door

Slams madly, again and again.

I think of the mud that must be running

Over the roads that wind down the hill.

In the storm there is a voice, begging me to stay.

Baleen

Caitlin Jackson

The women in the village fish from the stream
with water running through their teeth like whales.
When they catch one, they toss it to shore.
The more they bend to drink, the thicker
their foreheads become. The smaller and redder
their eyes grow.
The mothers come, bringing their sons who shout
with joy and collect the fish from the soft banks.
They will eat them later
with glasses full of cold milk
for their growing bones.
The women keep drinking and tossing
the fish they will not eat. Their teeth become longer
and thinner. Their arms grow shorter and thicker.
The mothers smile and thank them but do not meet
their now tiny eyes or peer to see into the water
flowing through them.
They take the small sticky hands of their children,
and the silver scaled twitching fish,
and they walk back to the village,
maybe telling a story
or singing a song.
The women still drink. At least the water
is cold and clean, and the mothers' singing
sometimes floats on the breeze
back for them to hear. Sometimes it stays in the air
for hours.

Exported Landfill

Meimei Xu

I've begun to see the dust on the floor –
in braids, roping underneath the bed and nightstand,
rooting in my wooden planks. Begun to see

this head of hair, graying and matted,
my living littering the country
like a slow sloughing, a peeling death,

my emptying my urn on concrete
and waiting rooms,
my outstripping my best.

It's a one-woman show –
the way I unzip
and crawl out of myself anew.

This is progress, our need to outgrow ourselves
day by day,
the fresh skin, metallic. Meanwhile:

yesterday's manias
shipwreck on the coast of my birth.
The children I could have been

pick at the deep back of a TV
for gold, their waters swimming
with mercury, the cancer

I should have had
breaking another family brittle.
I am not there, but here with the corpse I shed:

a map with no X, a trail charting the restless felon.
The old self, disowned,
is waste. If my lifetime

a wasteland makes, then show me
to degrade – Should I burn? –
Or perhaps,

teach me to diminish.

Teach me to live
without wreckage.

Home/Made
Emily Somoskey

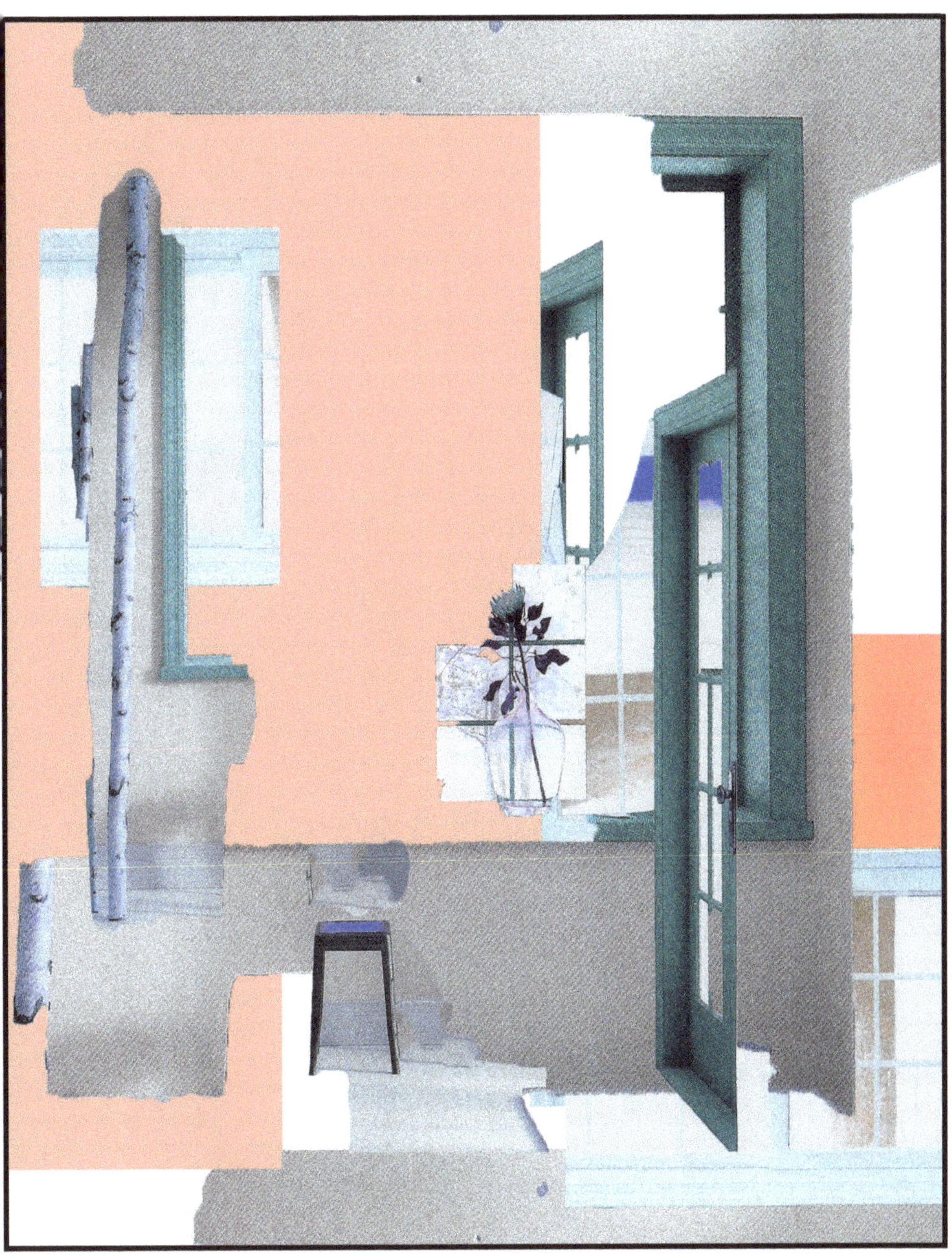

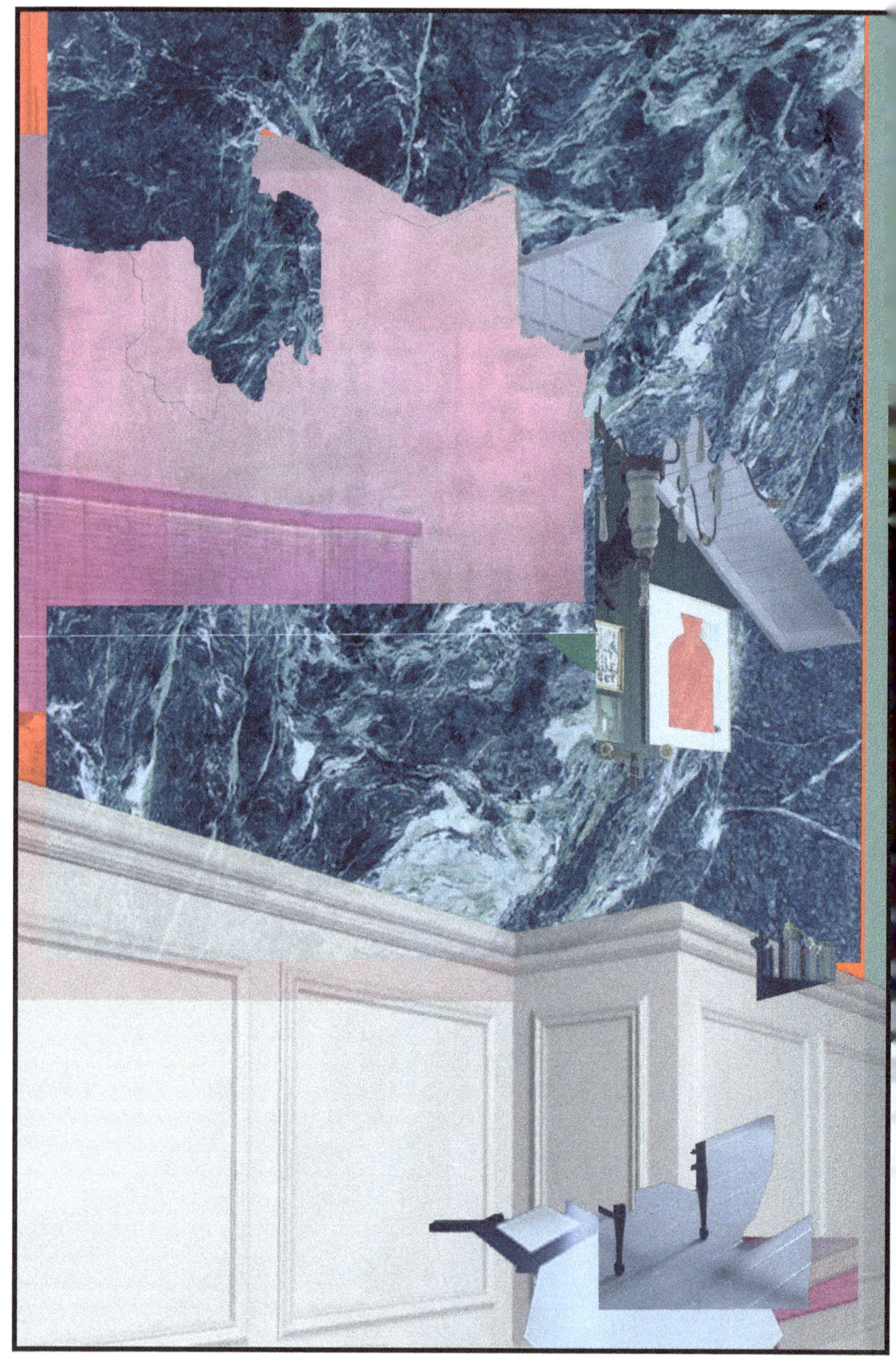

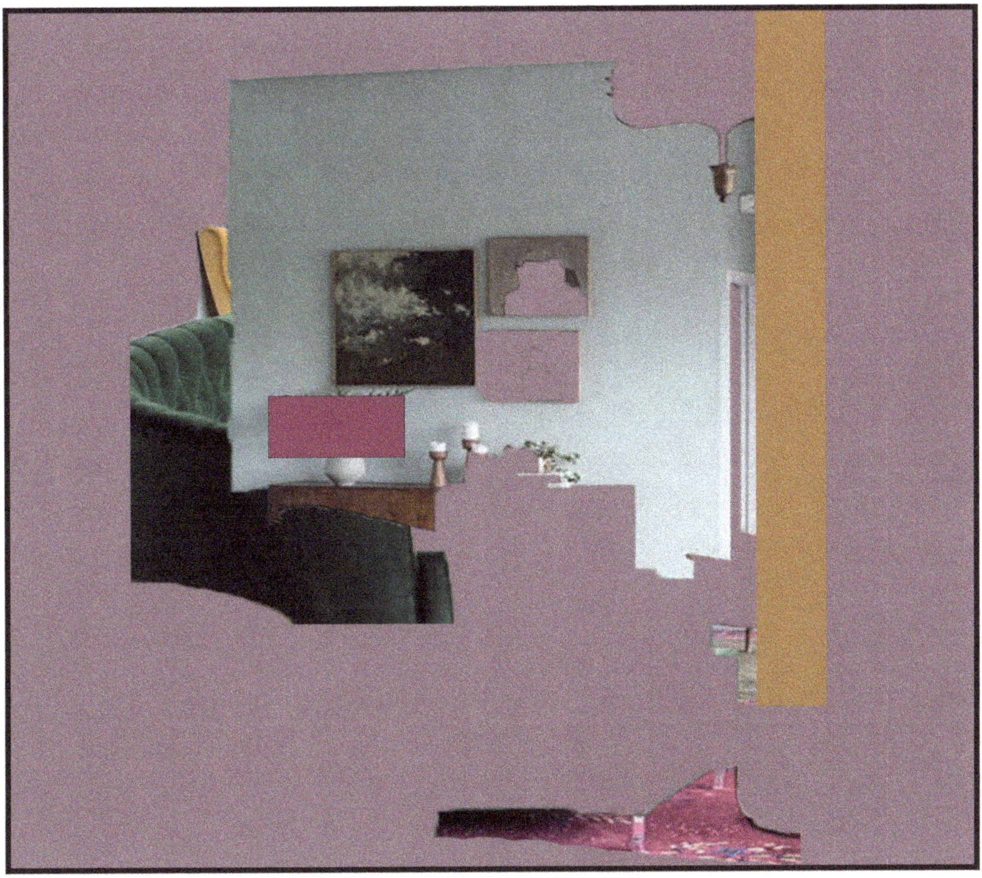

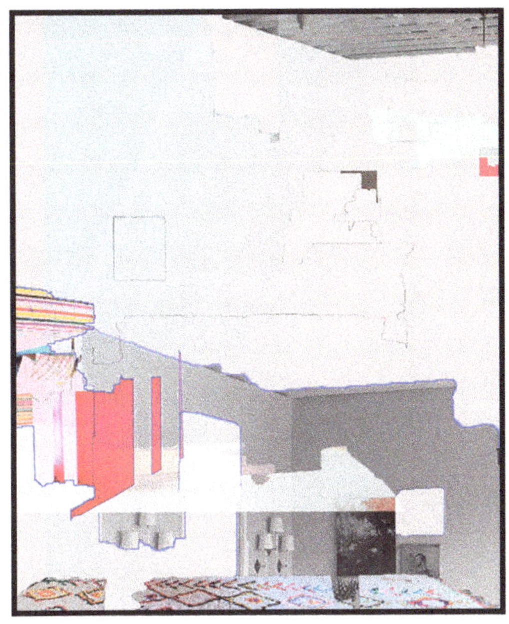

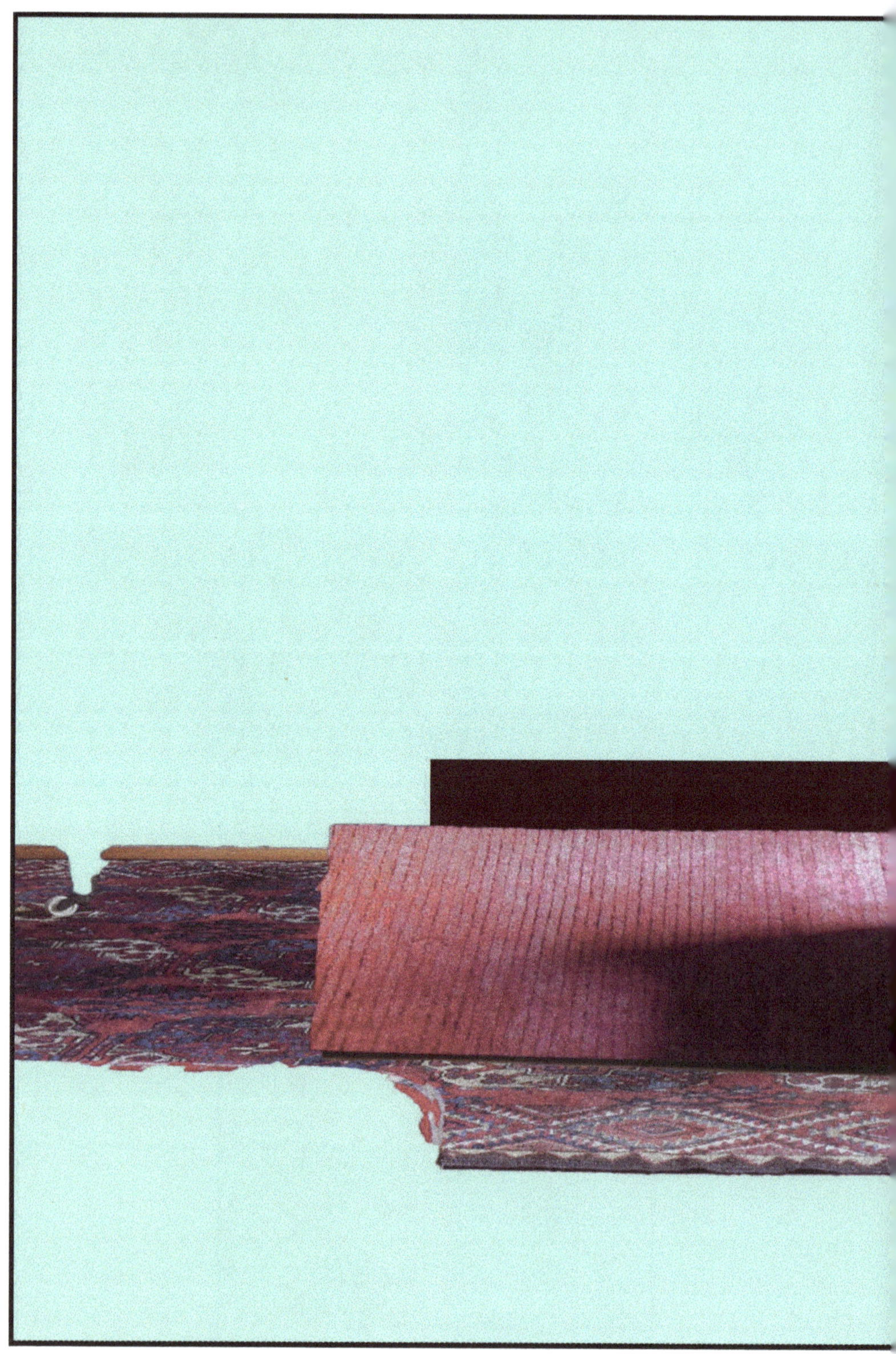

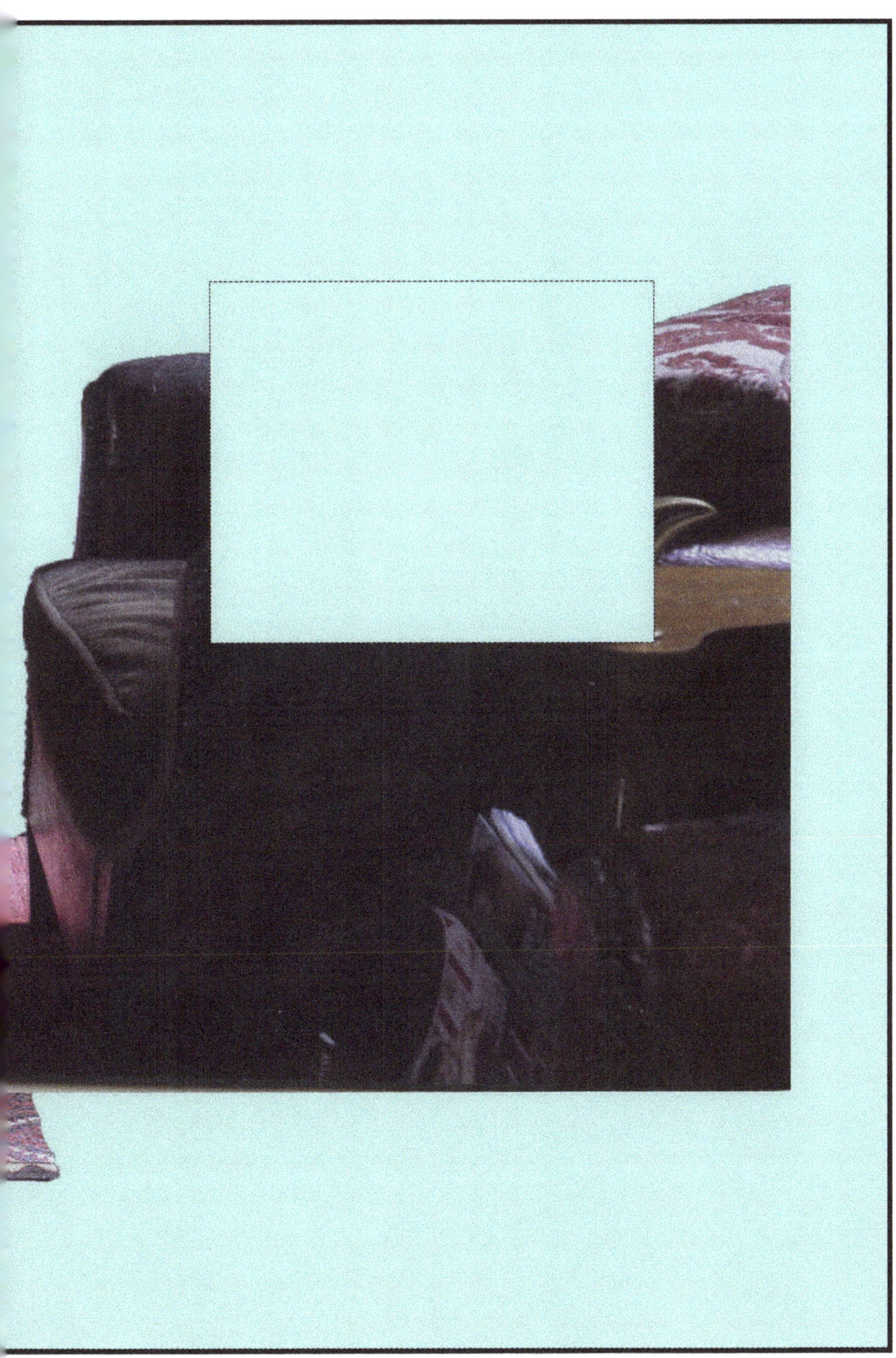

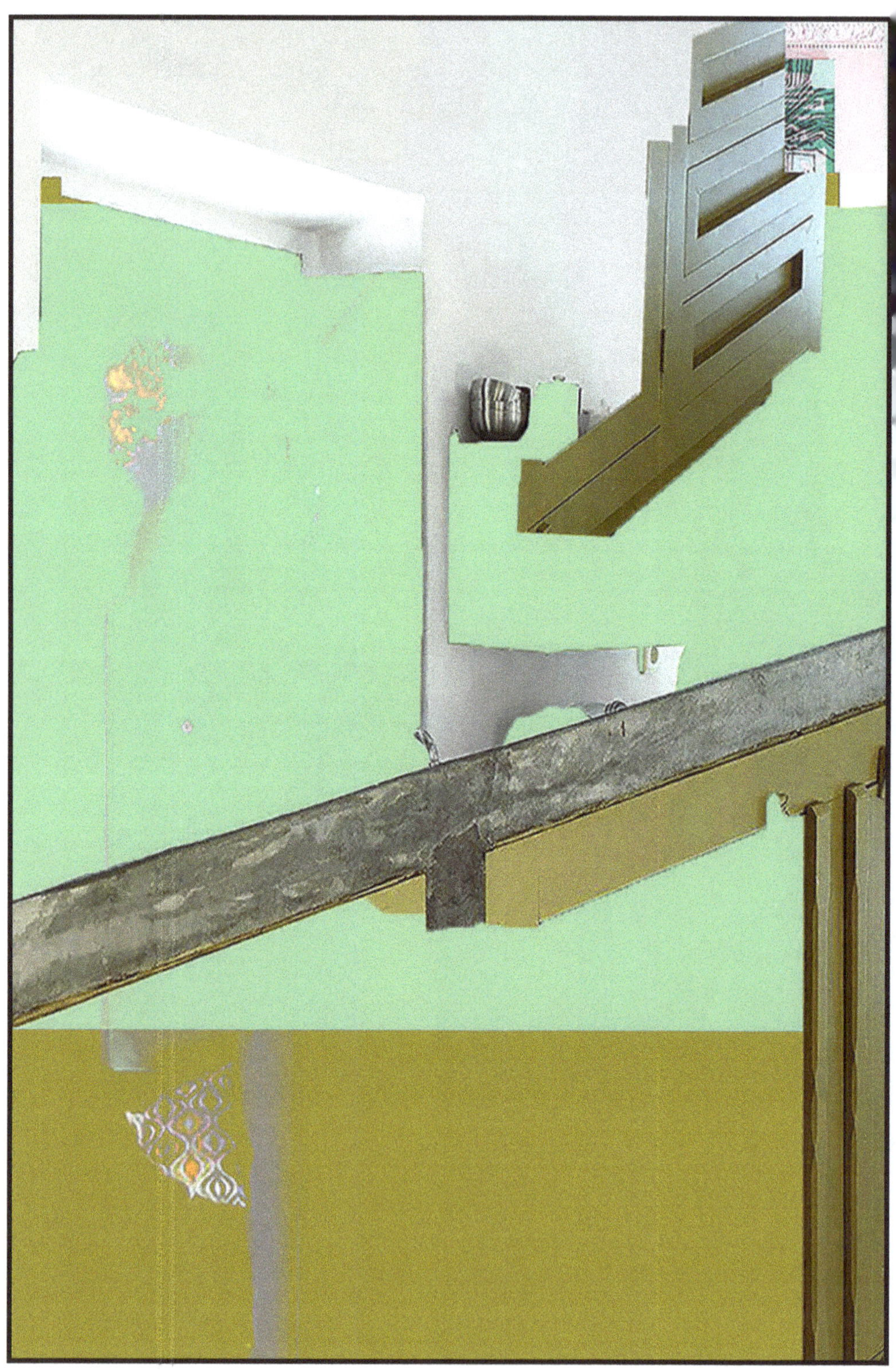

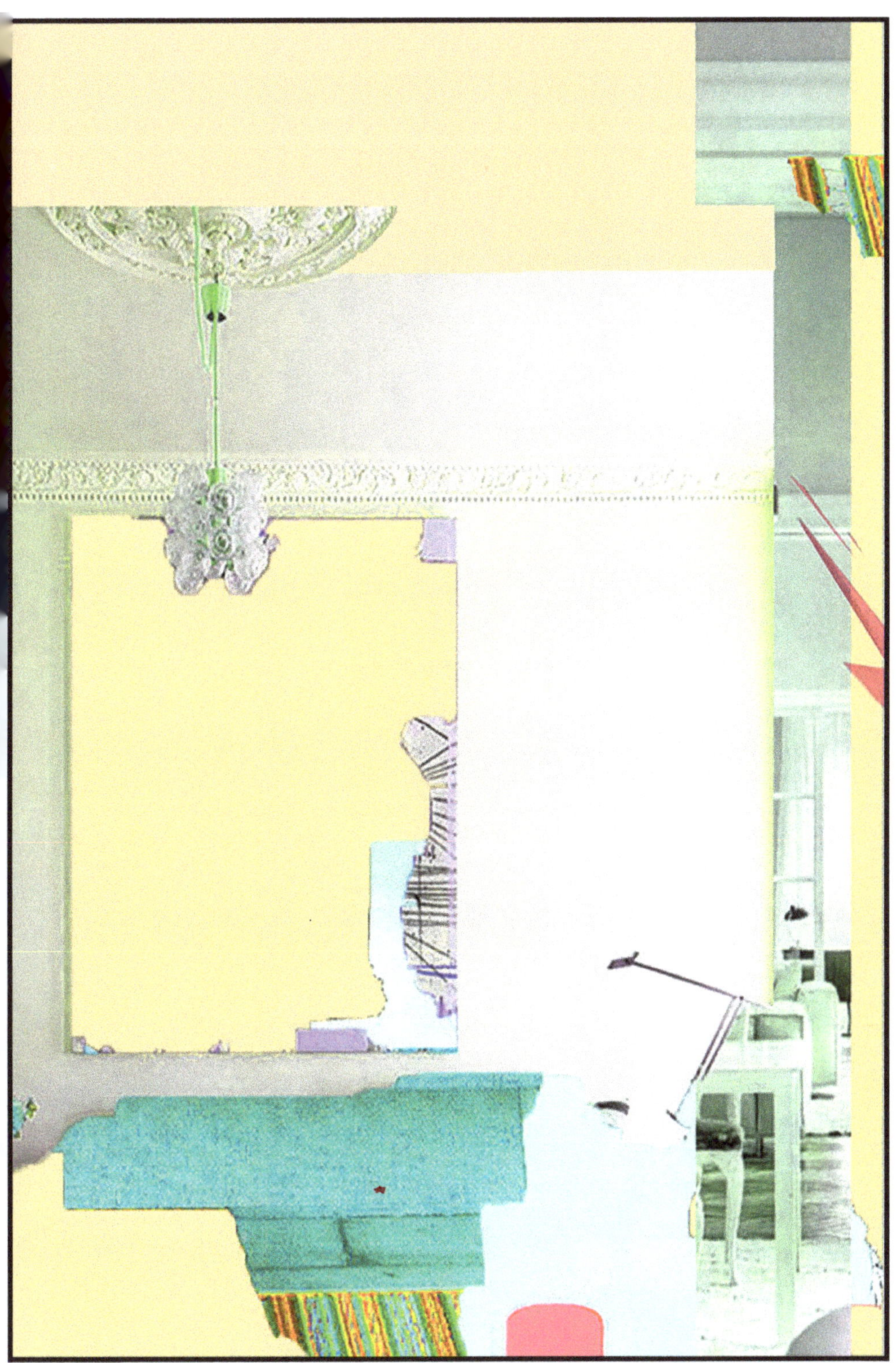

PRAYER FOR WHITE PARENTS

Elliot C. Mason

(PRELUDE TO THE DAILY NEWS)

be careful papa, pretty mama, step down
from the garden path where you plant
dead mint stalks and hide the cracks
in prayers for rain – your children are
not coming back. your teenage daughter
is using your favourite summer flip-flops
to spank a homeless junkie, and her
waxy ass is tattooed with the face
of your ginger cat, Pimples. your son
is storing heroin and wraps of foil
in his blue lapel, hiding needles
in his earrings and little gay lovers
in that rusty Ginsberg slate
he promises to read as soon
as the smack wears off. does your
teenage daughter smile at her grandmother?
she's using her for drugs
money, convincing senile elders
it's her birthday seven times
a year. does your son have friends?
he's sucking them off, munching
cum, he's thinking about switching
from law to cultural studies, injecting glue
and listening to The Doors. Mama, dear
dear papa, your children have changed.
choo a-choo
> *clap your hands*
> *call in your saviour*
> *the local Tory councillor*
he was a BUSINESSMAN before this
> *and only took cocaine if it was*
> *strictly necessary for bonus profits*
> *he will fix it*
choo a-chooo
> *like he fixed tax loopholes by*
> *stuffing them with money he*
> *stole from ducking tax laws*
papa, mama, wipe your hands of that
cupcake dough, put down the remote,
it's all on repeat anyway. come out

to the world, it's wonderful. your party
is in power, all your children have died
overdosing on bumsex and sad slow rock.

*look at them enjoying it, emptying
the pension pot, merrily painting austerity
onto open futures, shaking their shiny heads.
i wish i was old like you, i wish i was
terrified and bald and in the constant
comfort of fear and hatred, then i'd love
this century. i'd be so content, so furious.*

The First Time I Read Harry Potter To You

Monica Stevens-Kirby

It was a night I tucked you in,
pink and soft,
from your bath:
lavender soap and a warm water rinse.

Your eyes, like planets, little Neptunes,
swirling, round a solar system,
captive of my face;
looks we saved to tell each other;
a hook to hang our secret secrets:
silly words,
sharing whispers,
and I stood at the window to catch your dreams.

Mothers and daughters,
soaking up tempers,
flared by suns,
fading out of
upright outlines,
forgotten now,
flattened now,
into rest and respite, now.

In easy form,
your body gave
to cool, crisp sheets:
purple ponies.
Your pillow melted
with still-damp hair.

At sundown, I threaded my arm
around your neck,
gone limp, and
settling with the hush of dusk.

The moon was high,
but not yet full.
I saw one star and made a wish.

A story of a wizard boy,
his loyal friends,
who hovered there,

like the mobile from your infant nights:

pulling our eyes,
half-moons still,
backlit by a galaxy,
all ours for now,
to grab or stare,
to keep or stash in
blanket forts,
with books
and stories
(and flashlights.)

Transfixed, we were and hoped to be.

It wrapped us in a mist so sweet;
so plain, it was that weaved us in;
it was the loom that knit our hearts,
happy cat and silver cradle,
strings so tight and yoked-soft yarn,
invisible cloak of quilted love and
smells and memory.

It was ordinary, and it was magic:
our balm of treatment trusted, true.

Your eyes, like planets, dripped to stars,
sped up time and slowed me down,
fast-falling through the atmosphere and
freeing what I could not see;
the faraway light I stopped to notice,
lightyears after,
when it reached me.

Vacant Constellations

Haley Karin

At twelve I saw no beauty in well-lit adults

How they stargazed
next to their children
licking summer popsicles
down to splintered wood,   knowing
that stars made of myth
and sheltered in science
could shine long after light leaves

It's   really for the   best

               they say,

                I am happy with   all   this   space

      even though tears   freeze

        on their cheeks and

            their laughter
       doesn't make

        the right sound and

      pane after pane the darkness drifts on

         and on

        inside the galaxies

           of these ink-bled homes

                hollow

                  and   un-ending

An Exploration of Human Fragility
Mizuki Nishiyama

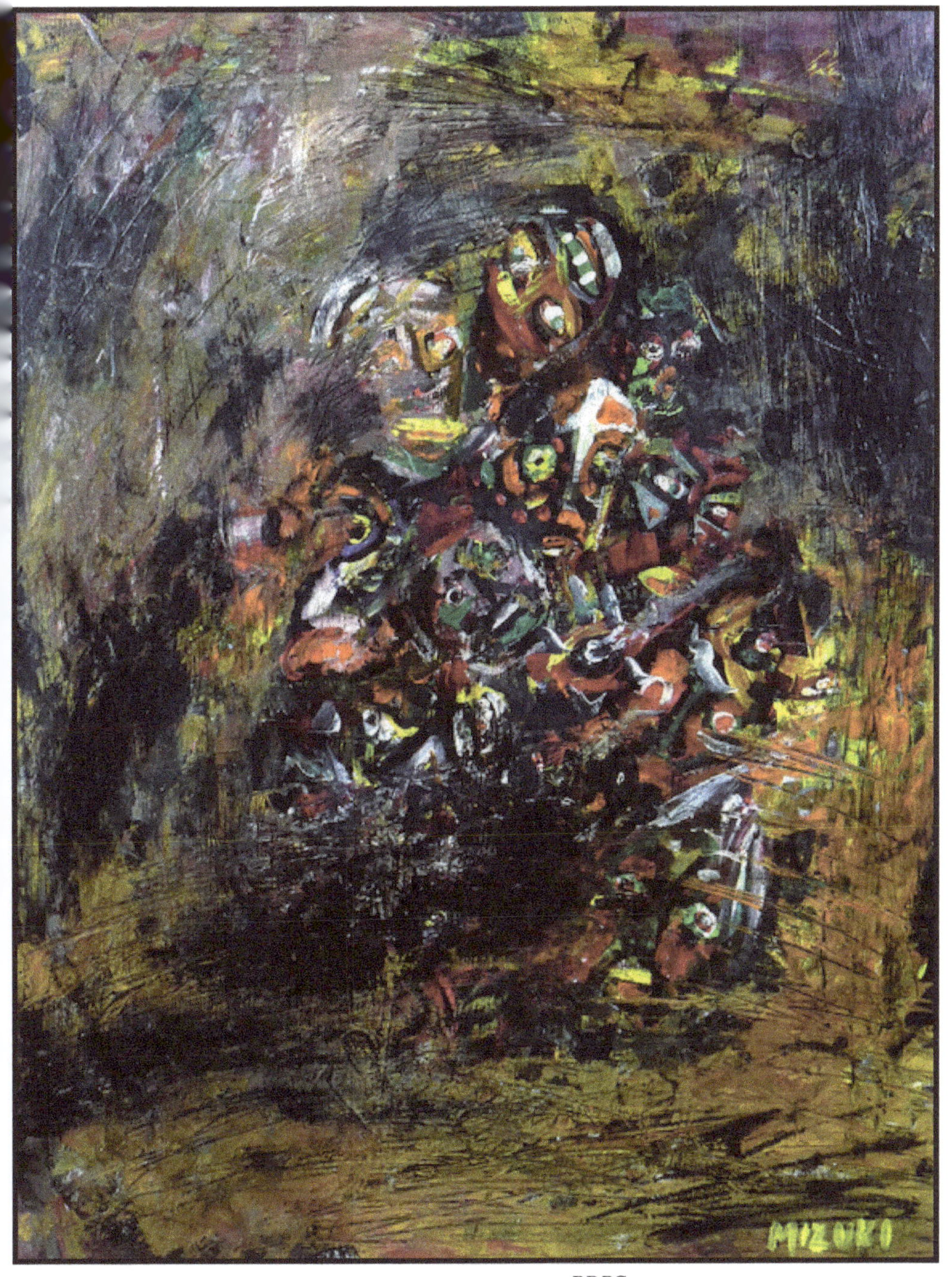

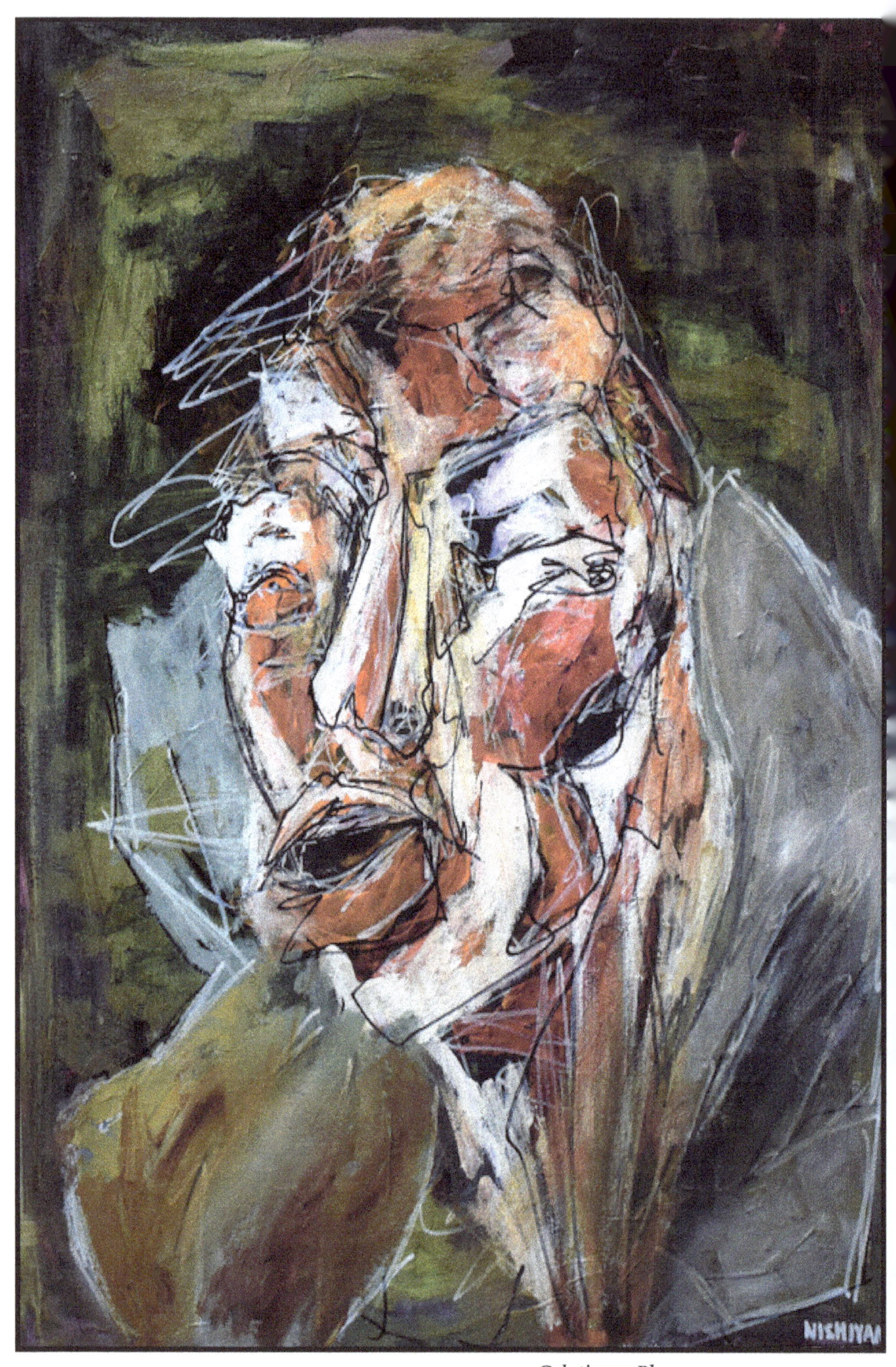

Gelatinous Bloom

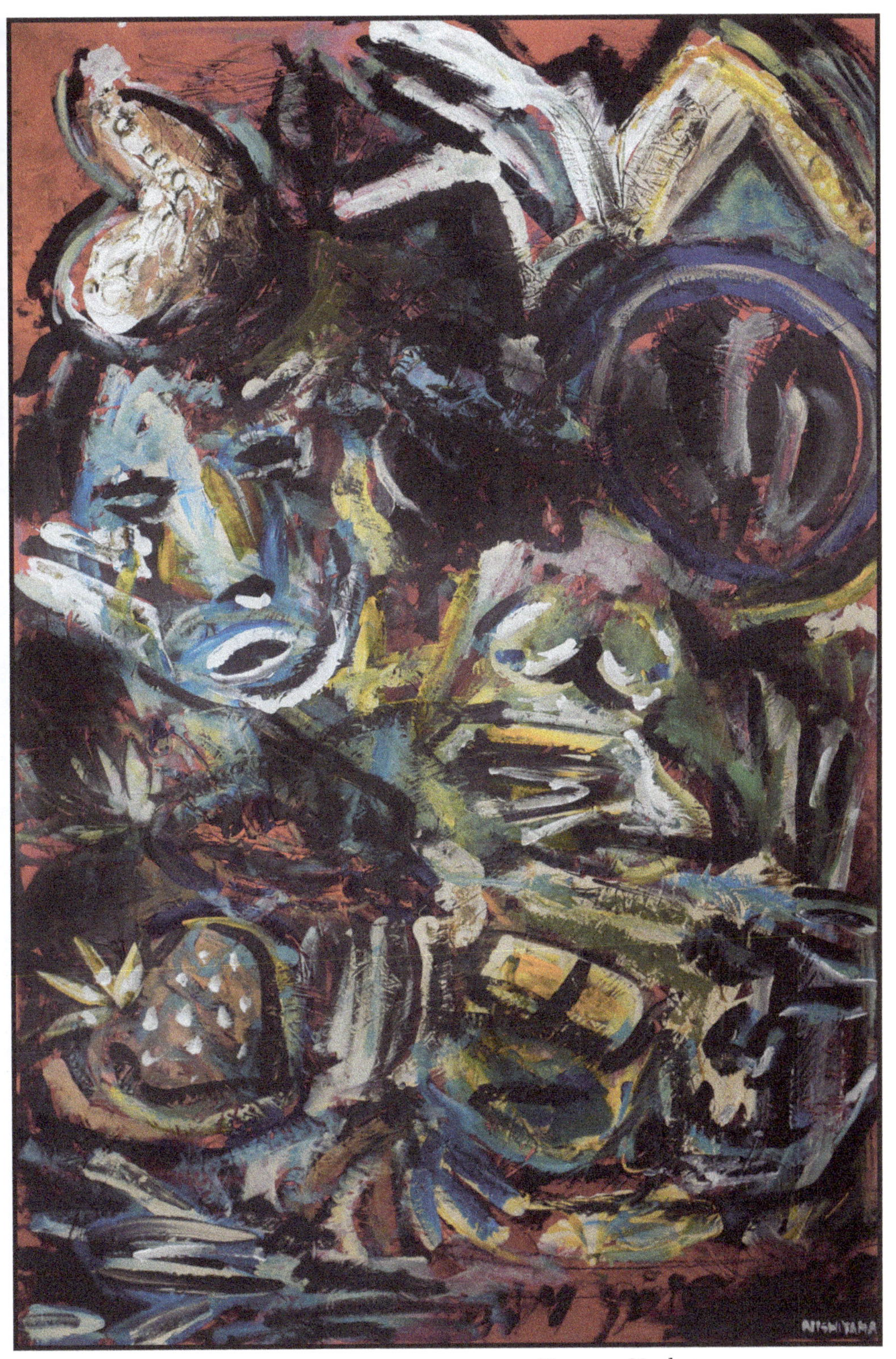

Moroccan Monkey

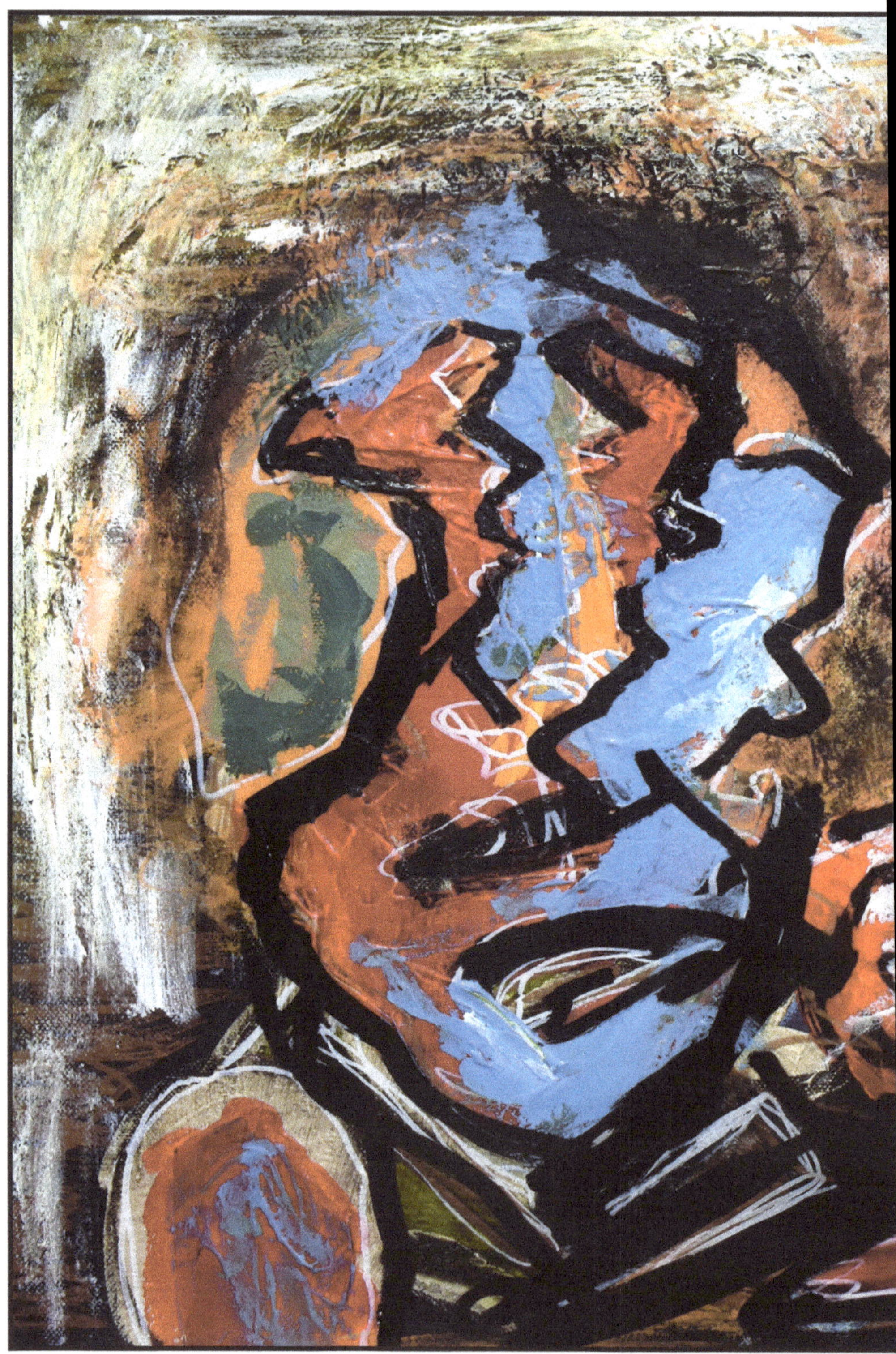

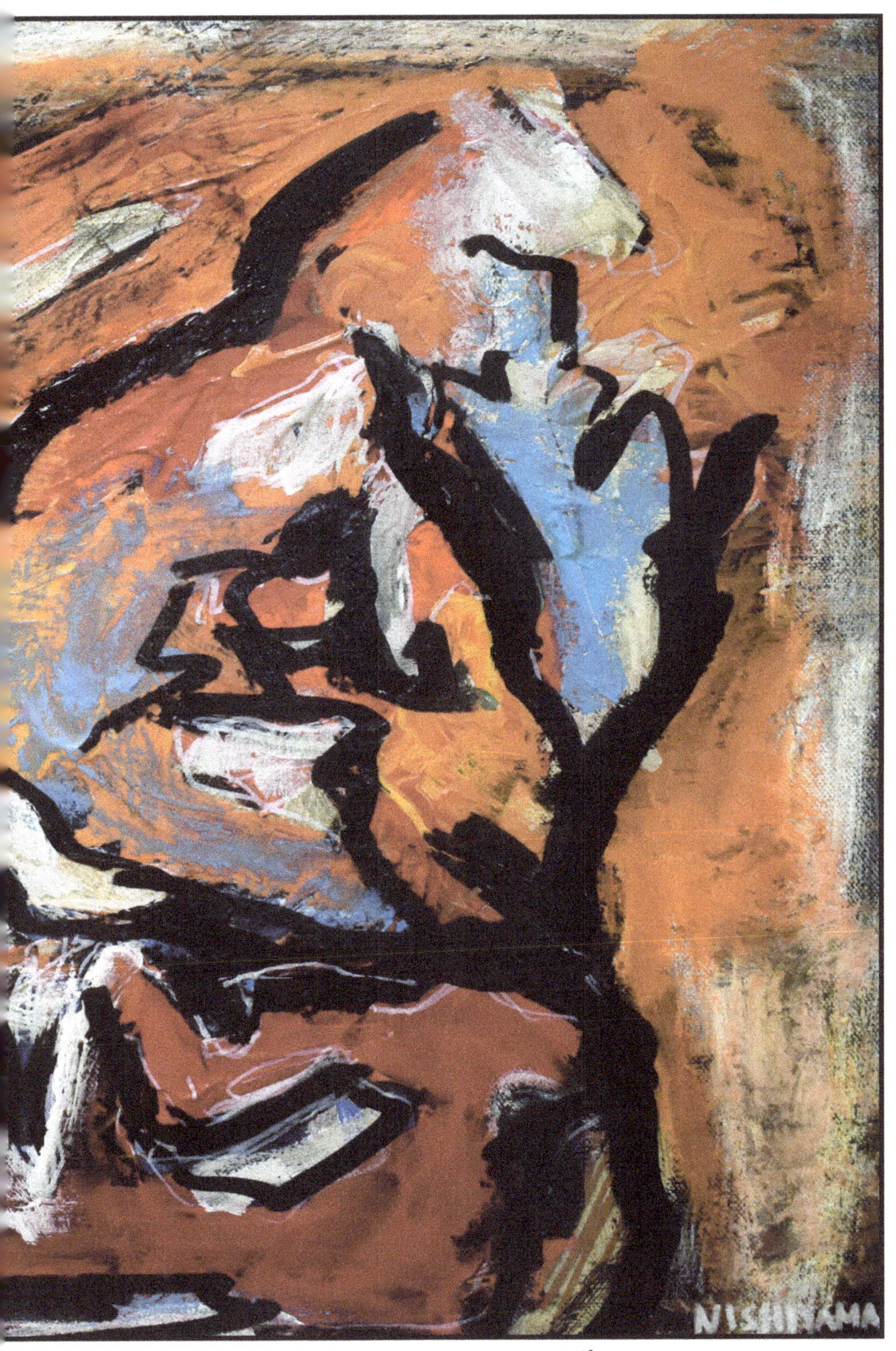

3 Chrome

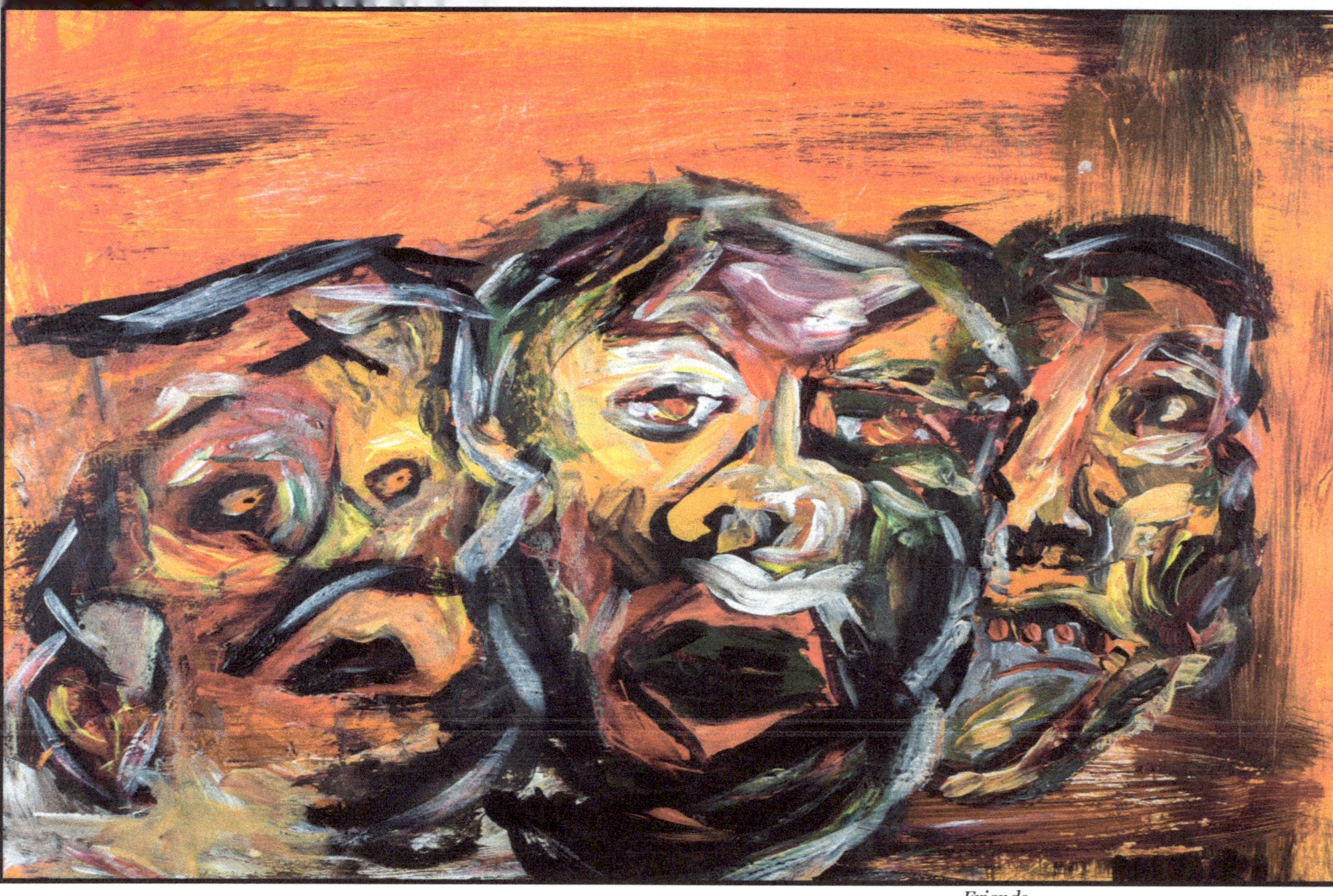

Friends

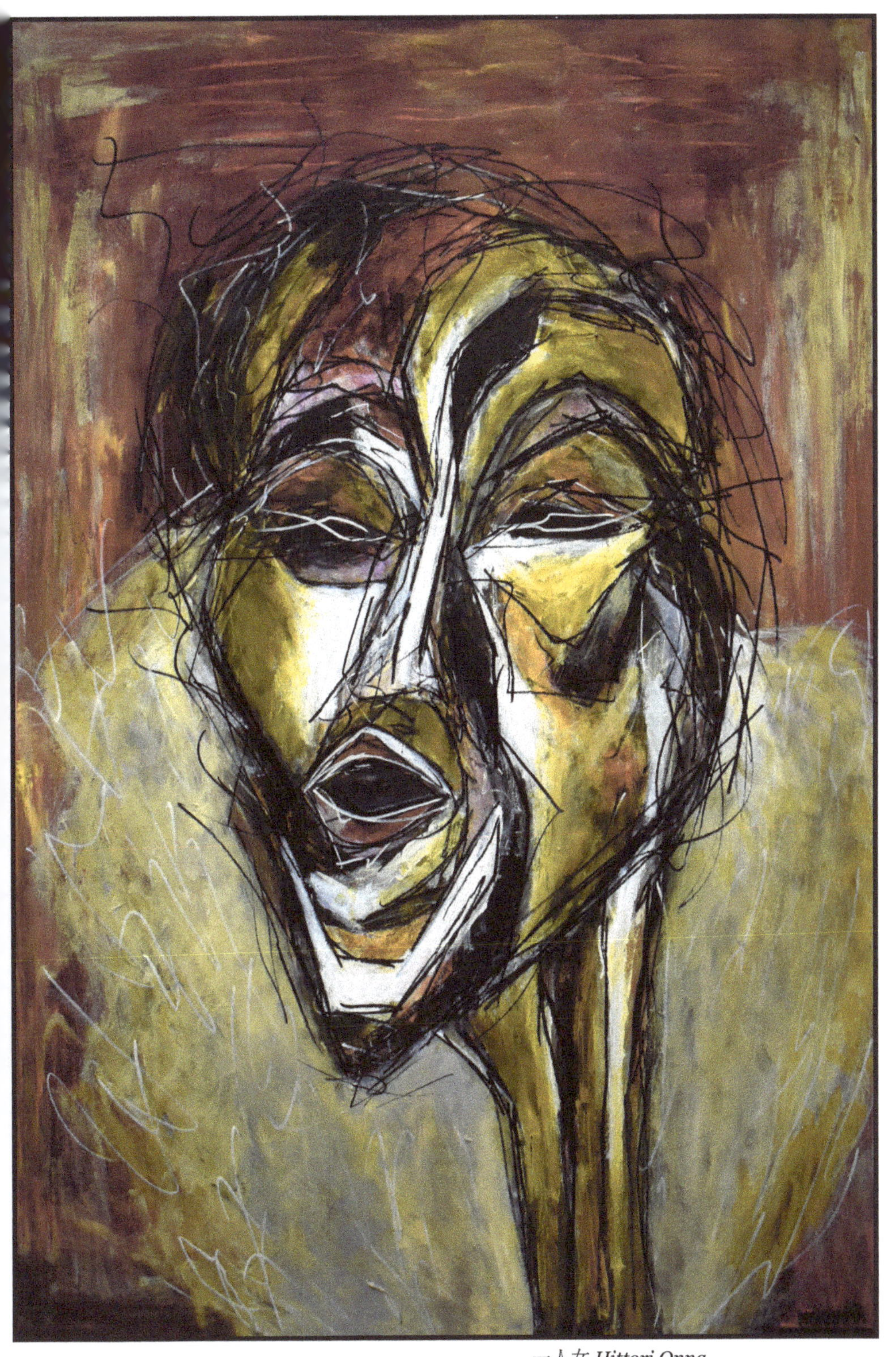

一人女 *Hittori Onna*

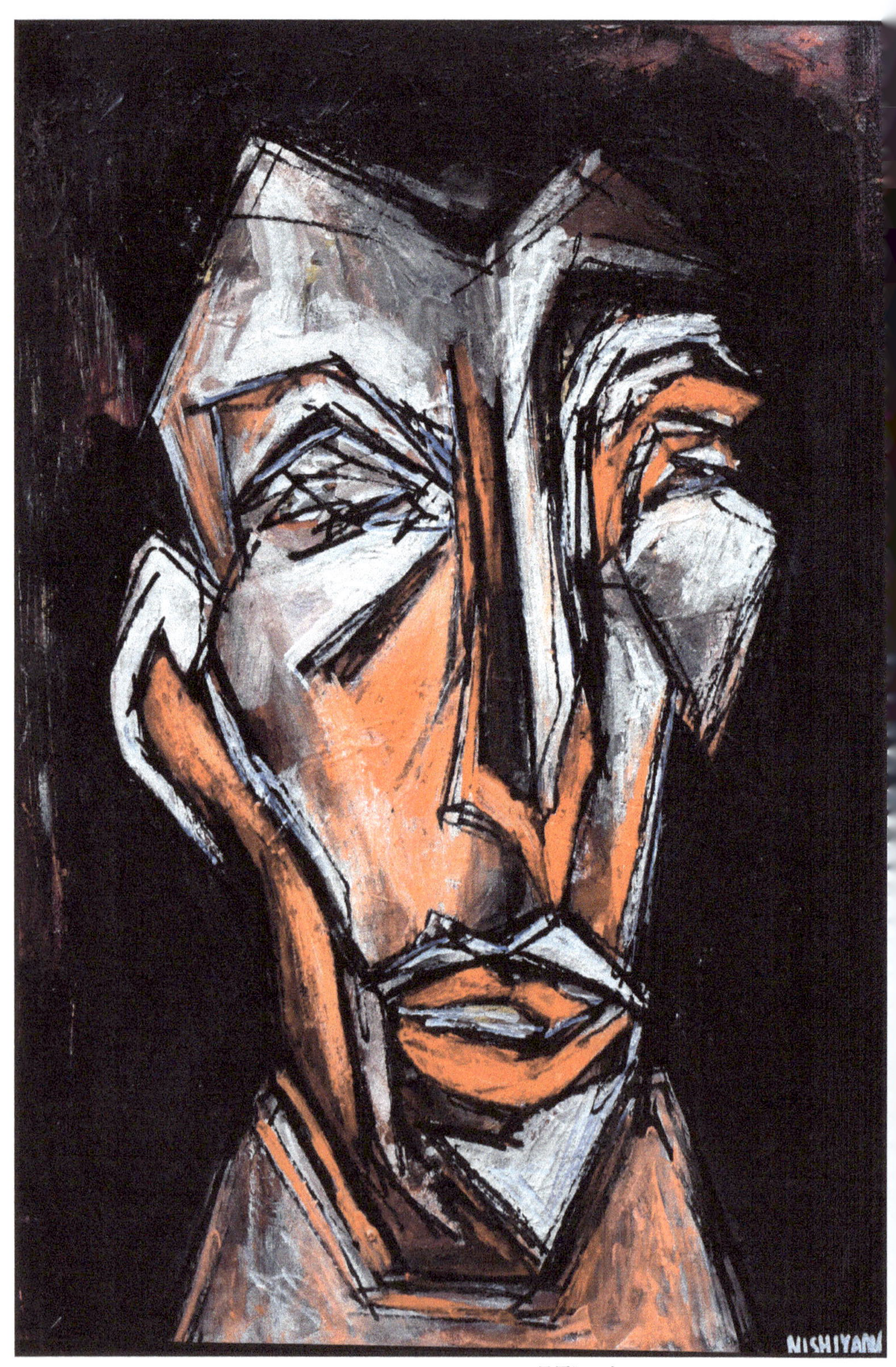

目優しい人 *Da-Ke*

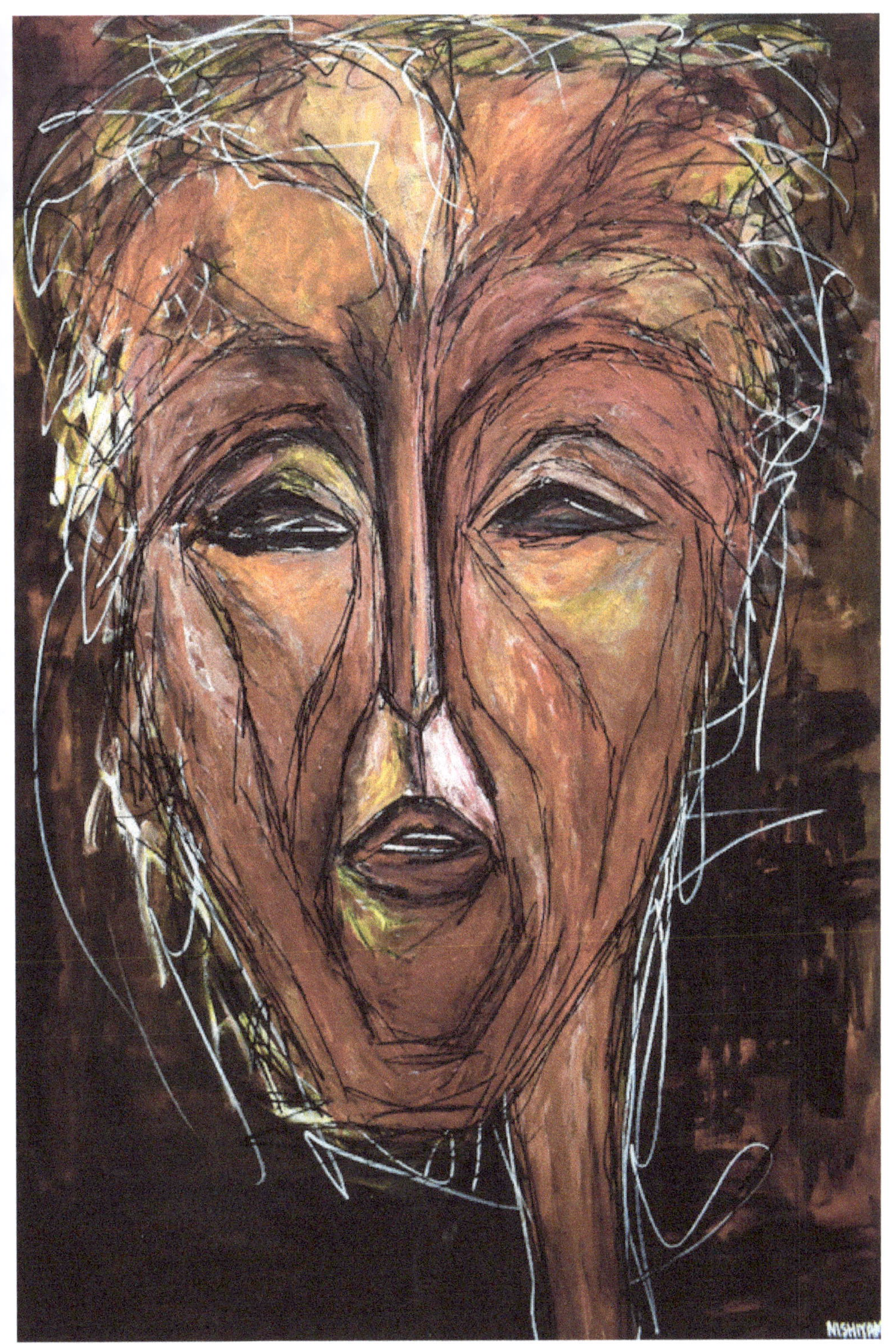

Swollen

BEYOND THE WILD BLUE

Nancy Reilly

Group us beyond the flat pictures of calendar time,
Beyond such a sweet bunch of numbers,
Beyond all running for the one that came before the aftermath,
Group us beyond the end row of Michael's rowing,
Group us beyond art for arts' sake,
And death for whose sake?
And who is not forsaken?
Group us beyond the genetic whorls of infants, pushed out, screaming into air,
Beyond the lining up, the rows of stripes, zig zags, bum steers, endless highways,
The countless short answers,
Beyond the rhetorical bru ha ha of found knowledge,
The digital die herds
in numbering markets,
Shares in the stockyard of shadows,
Beyond sealing it in a can,
Standing it up for comedy,
Sending everything back to China,
Beyond statelessness, placelessness, sleeplessness,
Beyond all the dogs who played Rin Tin Tin,
and human animals present and accounted for,
unaccounted for, and dead,
Group us beyond the insatiable thirst for the unnamable,
Beyond counting on invisible quarks,

Beyond the tedium of readymade goods,
hangers, hats, Hallelujahs, and hate,
Beyond robot plastic wrapped objects,
Beyond boxes, and crates,
warehouses full of refrigerators,
pills in bottles, blister packs,
Group us beyond the matter of all substances,
Beyond waiting in numbers for any exchange ,
Group us beyond our heart pumping
brain bending faces,
and other infidelities of memory,
Beyond identification's whip,
the groping ape heart,
Beyond the crazies,
Beyond watching factories smoke,
the other night,

the next day,
before the day before the day before,
the day after,
Beyond seeking cross identities
with perfect strangers,
Group us beyond the north face of the far- fetched,
and the close up, the sidewinder, the screech out,
time-space, the cold and dark look-up,
Beyond finding something meaningful to do,
Beyond waiting in the rain,
Beyond half-baked thoughts,
Back to front drunks,
Group us beyond heading for the wrong side of the tracks,
the first day of endless rehearsals,
the boredom of evil,
drugs of choice,
measures of ubiquity,
spotless formalities,
the bunnies in the wood hut,

Beyond counting on the power of attraction,
the violence of genetically erected fences,
of not forgetting to turn off the light,
Beyond mumbling the holy grails,
the number of pygmies left on the side of the world,
Beyond whistling for the long gone,
rescue lounges, good ideas, cigarettes,
Beyond the alphabetic rapture buzzing in our ears,
Beyond the mumbling numb skulls on
earth's chicken planet hell,
Beyond the quarantined tragedies in recovery,
the faint blood in the writing on the walls,
Beyond almost making it out of
the five-year plan,
the ten-year marriage,
the always divorce,
the c word in car accidents, castes and classes,
Beyond all kinds of hell, alarm clocks, scheduled workouts,
Beyond respecting time measured repetitive activities,
Group us beyond punctuality, lateness, not showing up,
Beyond facing the truth,
the Janus faced swipe of lies,
Beyond memorized adaptable, expandable, and dirigible characters,
Beyond delusions and embryos waiting to happen,

Beyond the cartoon jiggered pathogens,
and hot hunks churning favored antibodies,
Beyond white cells going berserk,
Beyond the duty of care,
Beyond the slick of hypocrisy,
Beyond willful determinations of the third kind,
Beyond, 'Oh let's just have a cup of coffee, and talk about it,'
Beyond, 'What the fuck?'
the angry, molten, spewing, spitting, clutching at straws,
Beyond the insomniac camera rolling in the naked eye,
Beyond all the nano cakes
in a dog shit park.

Just beyond the sentimental markets for ole time sakes,
Beyond repeating ourselves,
Beyond the yearning in hetros, homos, metros,
Beyond the fine line,
the thin line,
the dividing line,
the frontline,
the first time,
the invisible line,
the hair line,
Beyond frozen frown lines,
Beyond the do not cross this line,
the vanishing shore line,
the next time,
the unknown line,
Group us beyond inexorable time,
the mediations, measuring disciplines, thinking twice,
the funny kin color of yellow bellied mobs,
the naked mole rats,
Beyond the number of pages, we have read,
haven't read, may read, may never read,
The maps we depended on, the vacant eyed adolescents,
Beyond the needy greedy,
the old, oh yeah, outta sight outta mind,
Beyond constructing a master plan,
the made up of show business,
Beyond the cards, letters, the tatters, and the feathers,
Beyond the shit of inability,
the taking responsibility,
Beyond the territories of our own making,
the washed up of big mistakes,
the banality of hindsight,

the oohs and aahs of momentary rapture,
the moving landscapes out the window,
Beyond the getting away,
the here again,
the where to now?
the out beyond,
the hum of engines,
Beyond the lost ones,
the sound stories,
the birdcage poets,
the run of the blood,
Beyond anybody else's sense of self,
Beyond Kentucky Fried Chicken,
and good ole Charlie Manson,
Beyond all types of ambitions,
Beyond this scratching across the absence,
the beautiful and the can't think,
Beyond the California homeless,
And however many fish there are in the overbearing liquid,
Beyond the pencil tap, and what keeps coming after rhythm,
Beyond the green of going viral,
Beyond the unfathomable silence in snow,
the lucidity bite of solitude,
Beyond the lure of the sotto voce,
Beyond what other people could do for us,
what I could do for you,
what you could do for me,
Beyond all knowledge = sum,
the rhythm and blue in methadone, metaphor, heroin, cocaine,
Beyond the steady secretions, secretly parceled and accounted for,
Beyond what can't call out in illness,
Beyond the whir and blur between heads and machines,
the wet stuff, the dry stuff, the invisible stuff,
Beyond anybody calling the kettle black,
Beyond a picture of us without math,
Group us beyond the brief, insane, crazy, episodic shocks of perception,
we can't and haven't and won't really count on,
Group us beyond this sanctimonious listing of figures to ground,
Beyond fucking up and fooling fools around,
and the mumbo jumbo wagon load of lessons,
instruction,
invention,
history,
medical prescriptions,
scientific breakthroughs,

futurology,
scientology,
waiting in the wings,
Beyond this space of lettering,
Group us back to back,
from nothingness and the imbecility of rhyme,
Group us beyond why I haven't seen you in such a long time?

Earthly Delights
Meggan Joy

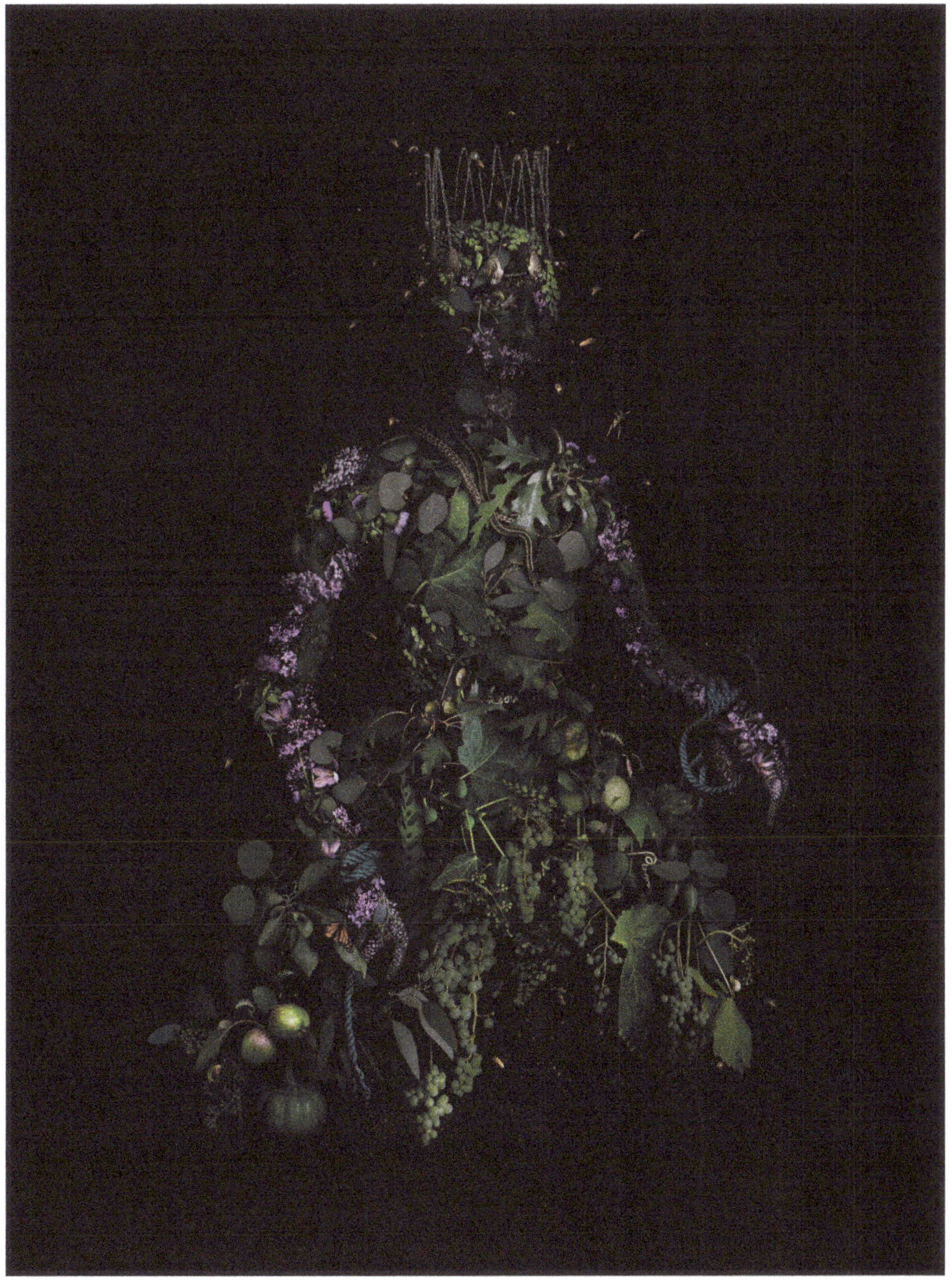

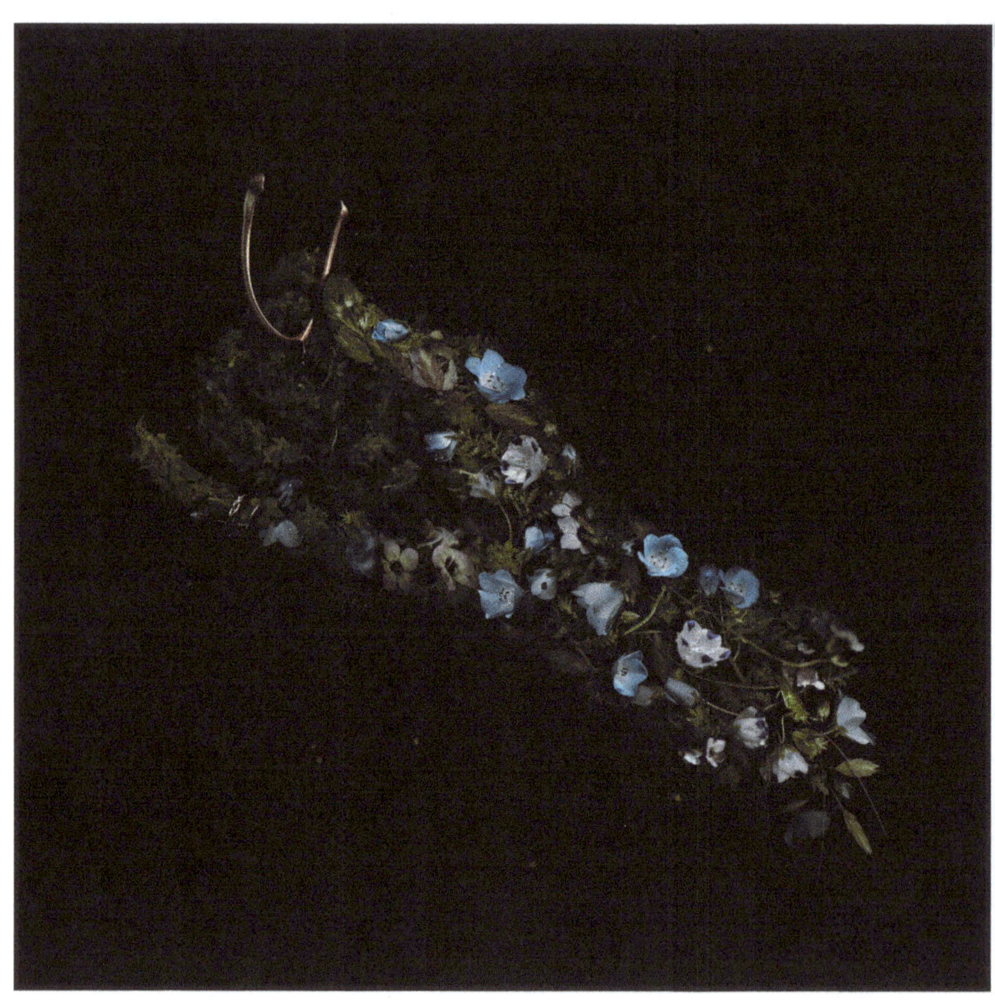

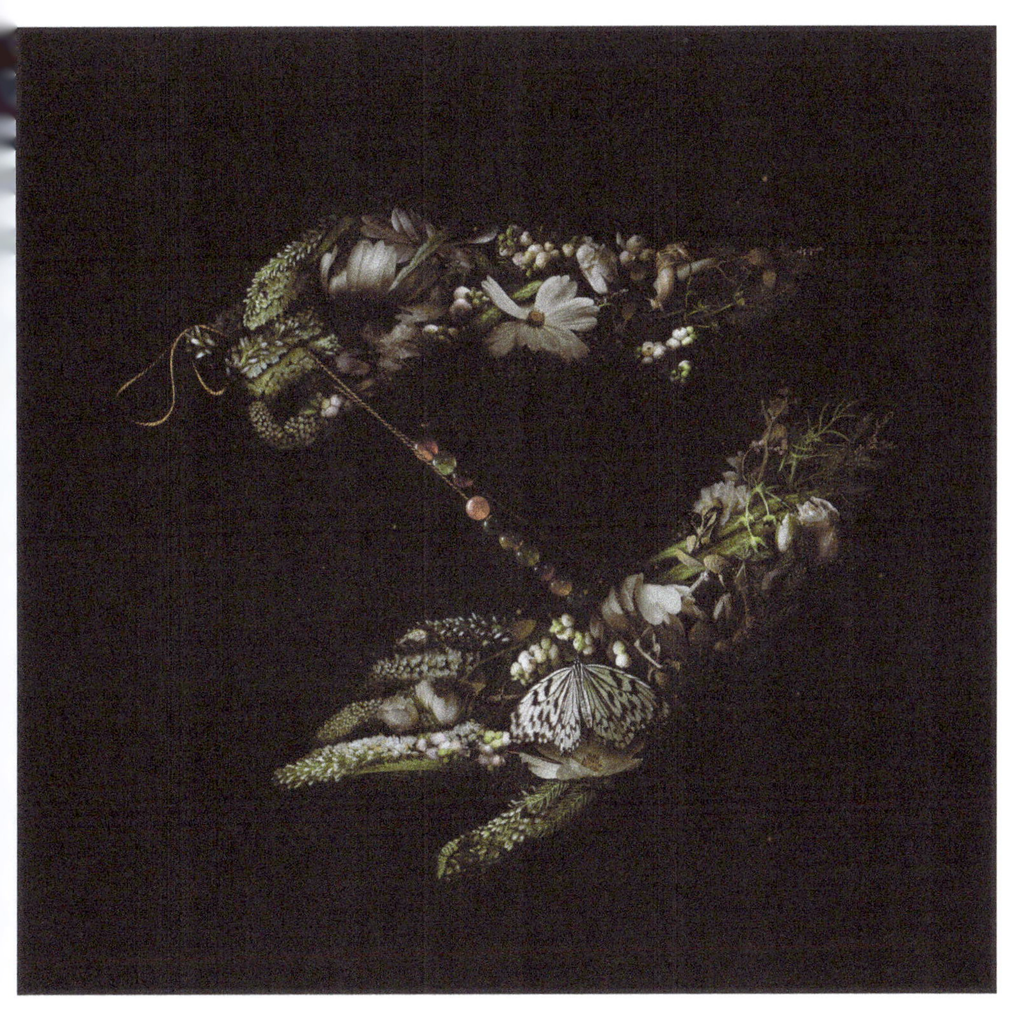

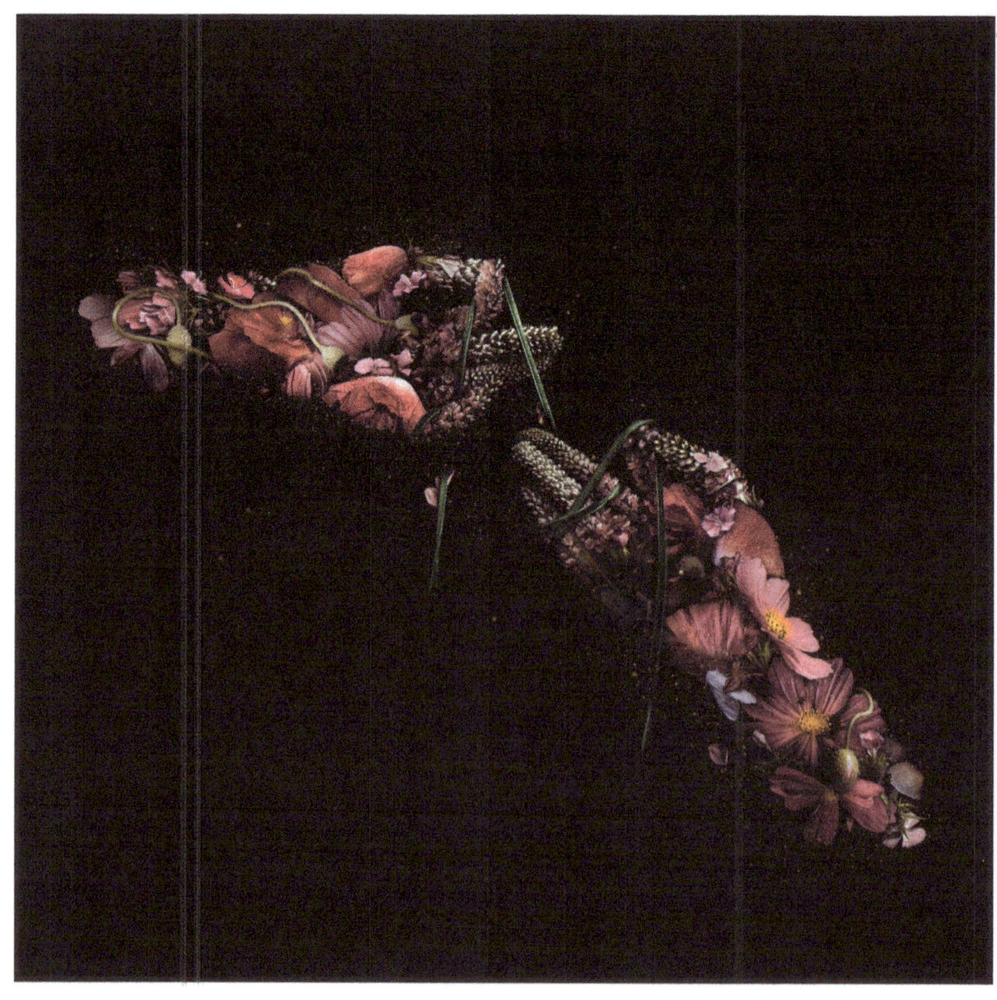

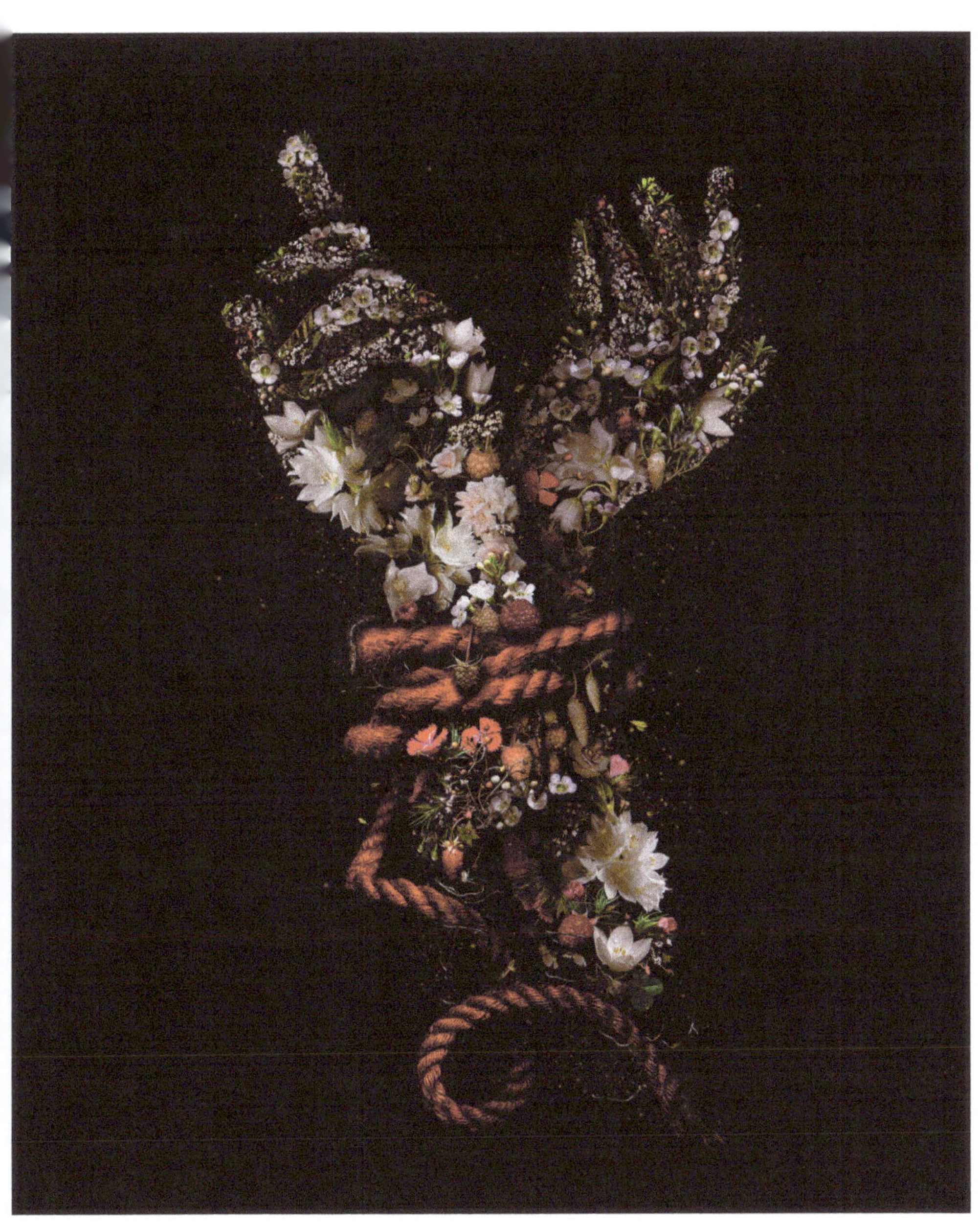

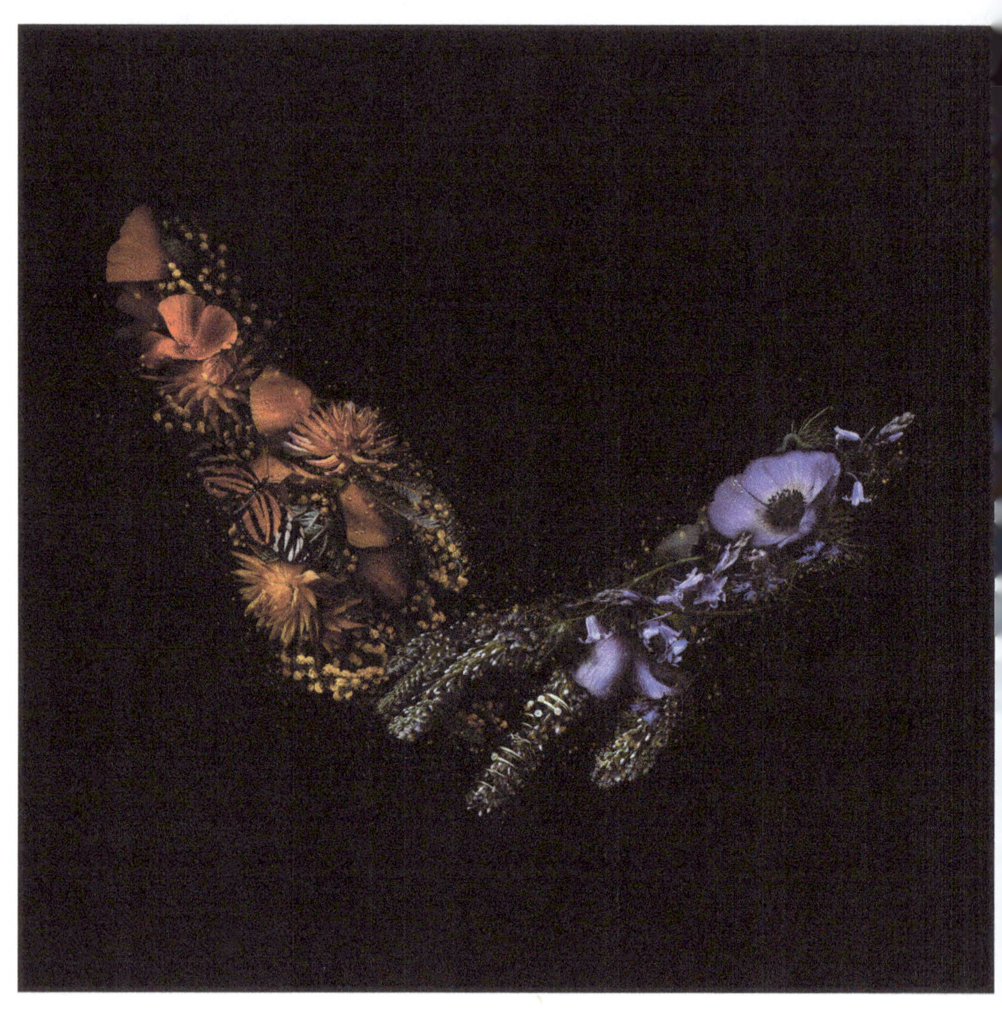

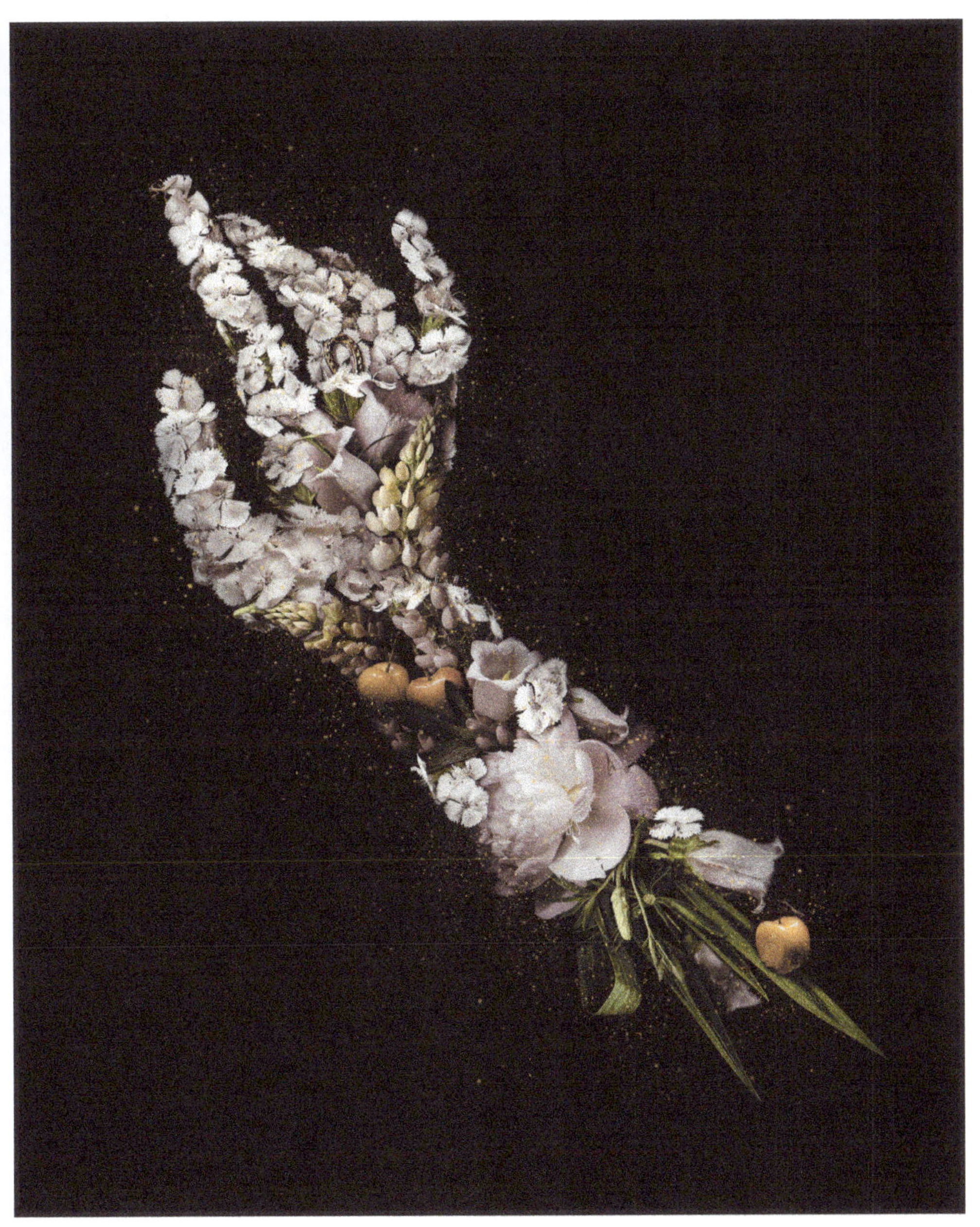

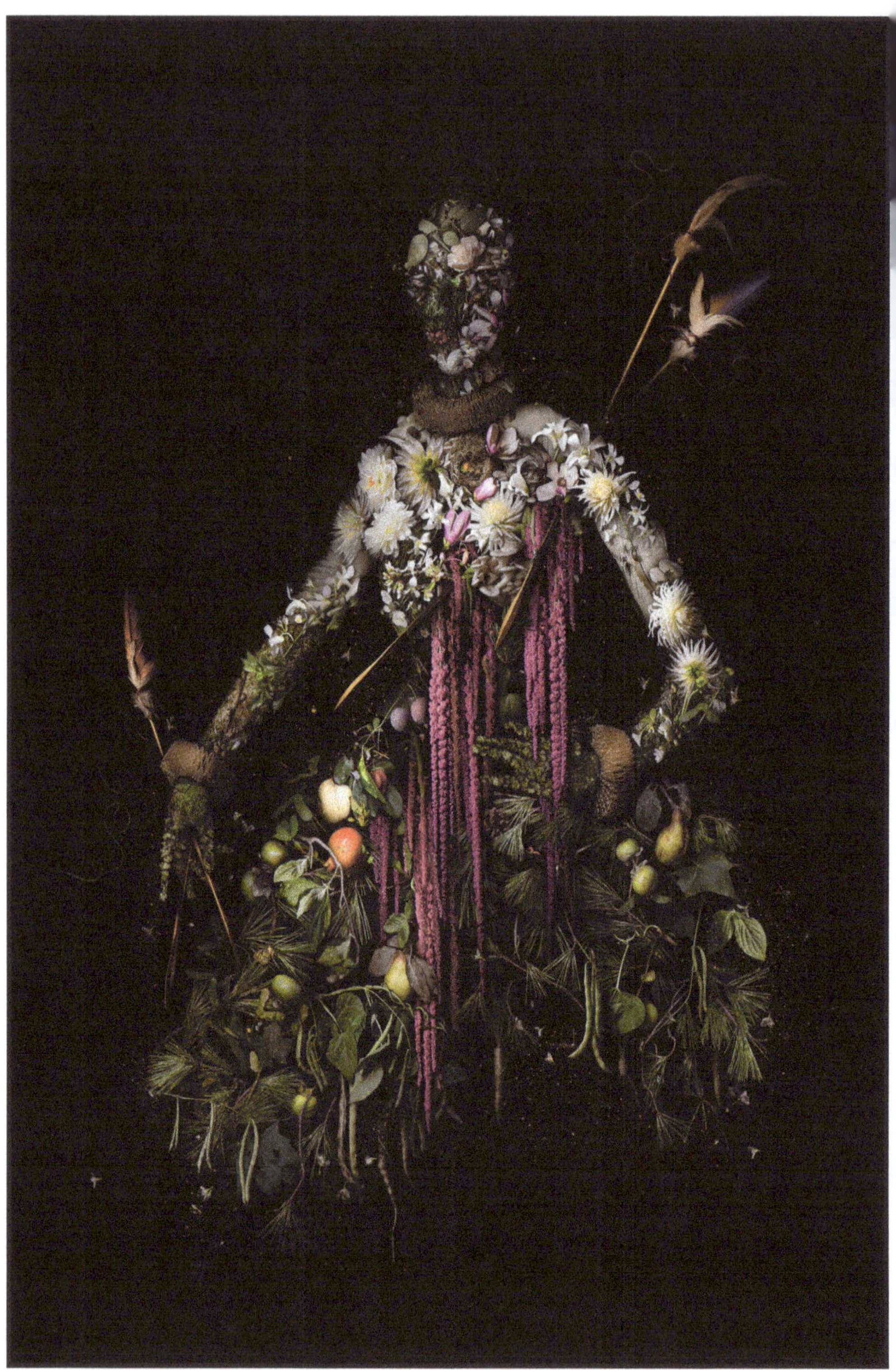

Job Oedipus Lear (David Achilles Othello)

Patrick T. Reardon

Dung dark lone.
(Lust flow betrayal)

Bible Greek bard.

King launches daughters to death.
Leper badgers for answers Deity.
Womb-returner holds, unseen, his eyes in his left hand.

    The baby dream of Agamemnon:
    Rage.
    Never show the scream. Their rules.
    Black,
    fetid guilt, a baby's blame.
    Small.
    Hell dark. From the sky.
    Afraid.
    Awaiting prophecy. The rotting bodies.
    Augur.

Self-blinded with maternal stickpins.
Self-paupered by paternal blindness.
Self-corrupted by faith disease/serum.

(Arrogant wife-stealer, foe-dragger, wife-doubter)

I am picked and pecked by crow scolders.
I ask one too many question.
I lust for rest without death.

    Let my sorrow river current between banks,
    Lord Eternal,
    between fields I tend and reap,
    and bake bread, and break bread,
    warm as Grandma's kitchen
    where she smiled — the sun
    jeweling soil and dogshit and growing
    things and creeping things and
    the newborn and the dying and the dead.
    Her bread was sprinkled with flour.

Did Lear know of Job, Oedipus?
They would have recognized him,
having each made the same vain grab.

(David was caught in the war of his sons,
Achilles caught the arrow in the unwatered spot,
Othello listened with his ears and caught nothing.)

Job knew Oedipus guilty of
blind copulation and murder
despite innocence.

Oedipus could have chatted the other king
family dynamics until
the cows came home to roost.

      Under the train tracks seven miles,
      I take a step and
      the movement pulls my other leg and foot
      up and forward and
      this is the way it goes and
      has gone and
      will go until I take the step
      out the back door
      for my appointment
      with the gun.

My impatient patience.
My clutch for clear vision.
My miserable map.

(My hands on her pure throat.
My song to the roof-bather.
My gleaming blinding armor.)

You opened yourself to the whirlwind.
You self-crueled your blameless flesh.
You knew yourself a fool, nuncle.

      Translate breathing. Define
      the voices in the shadowed alley. Explain
      the tracks of blood and brain
      to the harsh pebbled touch
      of the cement garbage box

by the crab apple tree
where brother David wanted to hide. Be
precise about orgasm. Spell
the animal hoot. Cackle. Render
weightless steps. Construe
a poem. Pray in a line. Draw
a schema of anxiety.

Don't trust Job's happy ending.
Hear eye-castrated Oedipus.
Hug the foolishness of Lear dying.

In this life, innocence
dangerous as success, everything
to the same place.

Skin

Eimear Bourke

You're clean and functional
But so dry, so thin

Pellucid paper
Encasing my bones and veins

Written on you is all we've shared
So visible and obvious
You tell no lies

Freckled, hairy forearms
Scarred hands and calloused palms

You couldn't belong to a pretty girl who stays indoors

You're lived in and you're mine.

Barrier between the world
and
something that's simultaneously intangible,
yet familiar

Looking through your sheer shield
i can make out the vessels of my vascular

What is it you are holding?
Erythrocytes and plasma?
or some unspoken knowledge that you carry to my heart,
but not my brain.

When her fingertips touched you, you felt something
Something that the head doesn't realise it shouldn't want yet

YEH ISHQ HAI (OH, THIS LOVE!)

Shereen Akhtar

Ha, hai koi to baccha, jo jeena ka mazzah yun aane laga
    – Yes, can anyone save me, from the excitement of life that has
       come upon me?

5am & I want to get her coffee & she says sleepily
toothbrush & three days later we are side by side in the mirror &
shaking, a headphone each & mine falls out my mouth
& she tells me she doesn't know how to process the news &
when she leaves & I stay behind & it happens to us this time
& I take my colleagues to mosque to pray funeral prayer &
my 5am becomes powder & more powder &
I turn up to work shaking & see the table where she worked
& spoke to her rabbi about the book I gifted & I know
that wanting it to work wasn't enough & traditions weigh more
than hypocrisy & did I ever pray in front of her I can't quite
remember & I miss the smell of shabbat candles &
her long skirts & dream of it – a secret marriage & a new
5am routine & pesach & isha & a house full of complementary
interventions.

white-black snow

Steven J. Wills

(i)t has always been,
difficult;
searching, for
Love:

elusive.
running, like a
doe over smolder-coals in
dead-winter.

barren. life-
less, twisted-scarred
Trees; the White-Tail(ed) surrounded;
She, running through

low-heat remains.
spring brings things that
do not threaten 2nd &
3rd degrees.

Make the World Magic Again
Jenifer Fox

We wanted strangeness
redwoods falling upwards
communion with bees draped in tiger striped fur jackets
minding their own business
eating atoms
we were alive and buzzing free.
When she said *fungus* we lost control
her mouth gaping white as a mushroom moon
star teeth circling her serpent tongue
unregulated laughter, natural happiness
as if 2016 never happened.
When she said *truffle-sponge* and dipped her hands in mud
we melted into something sacred
the funny faded to gossamer
and we shimmered through the woods
golden auras stripped down to essential softness.
It took six hours to land again
back into the world that wants to deny
the magic of our existence.
Returning, eyes shrunk back to form
we sat on the park-bench and wept.

The Art of Gregory Fitzgerald Brenner

Gregory Fitzgerald Brenner

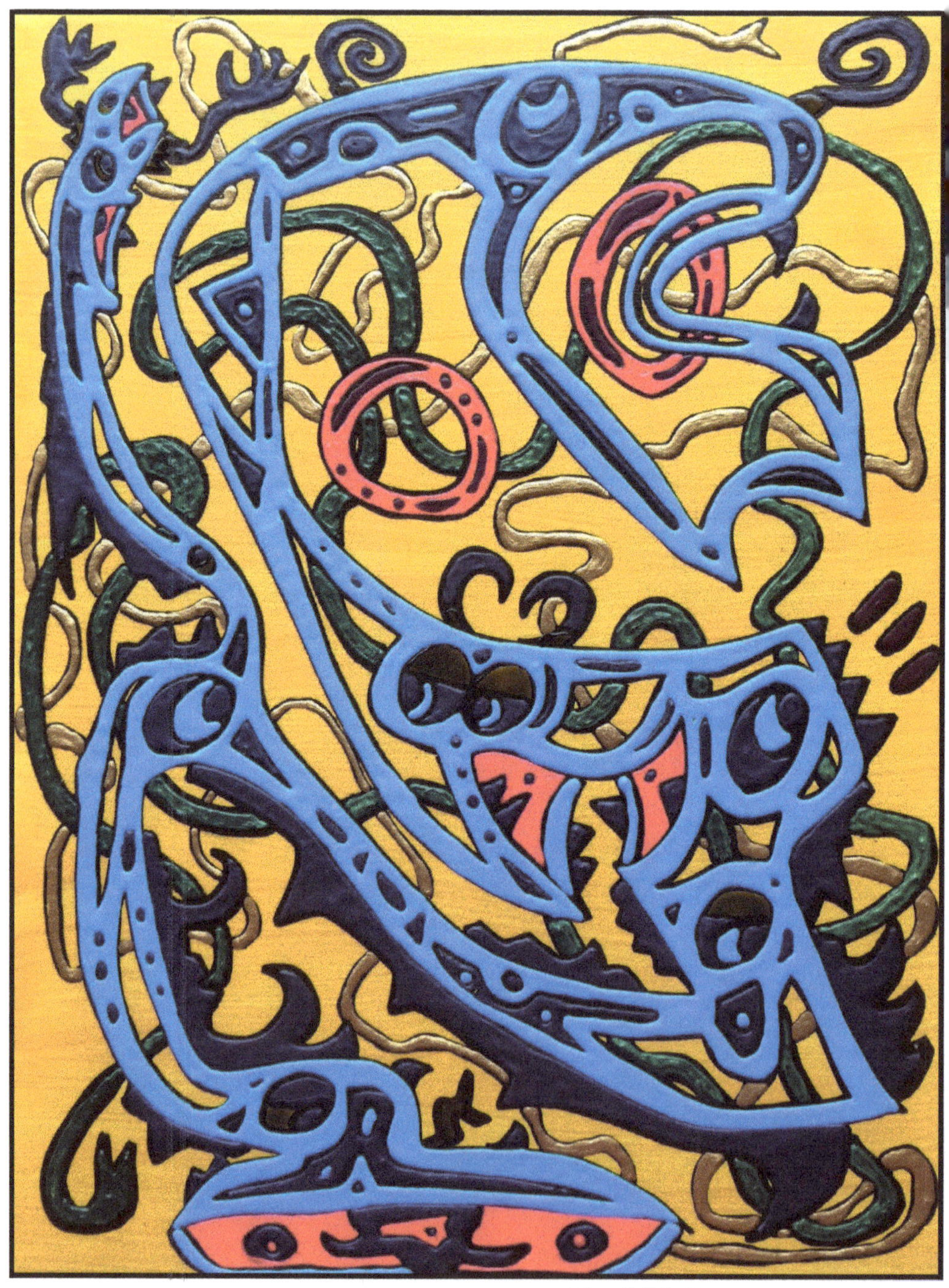

Ring Call In Time

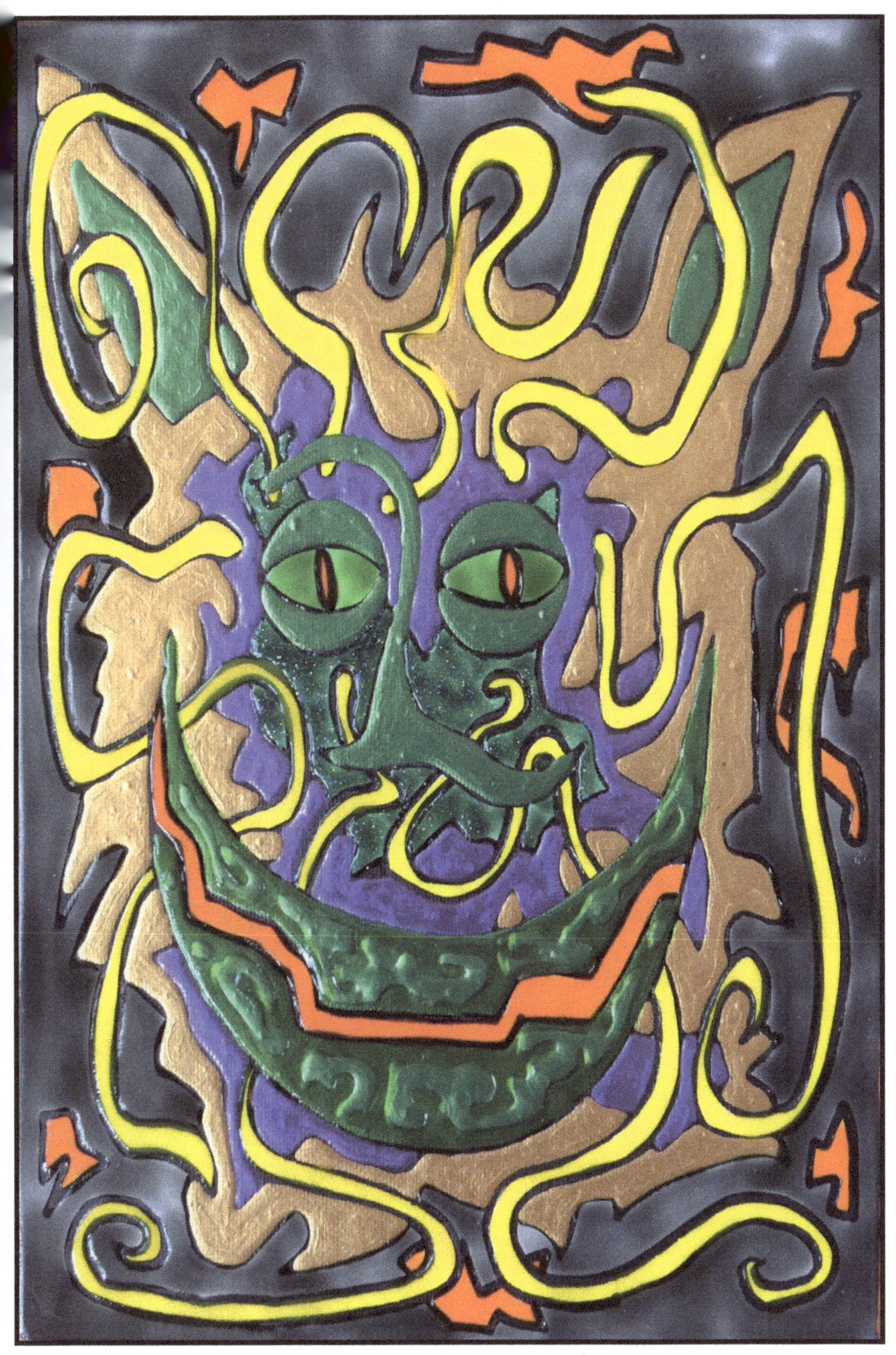

Smoke Scream

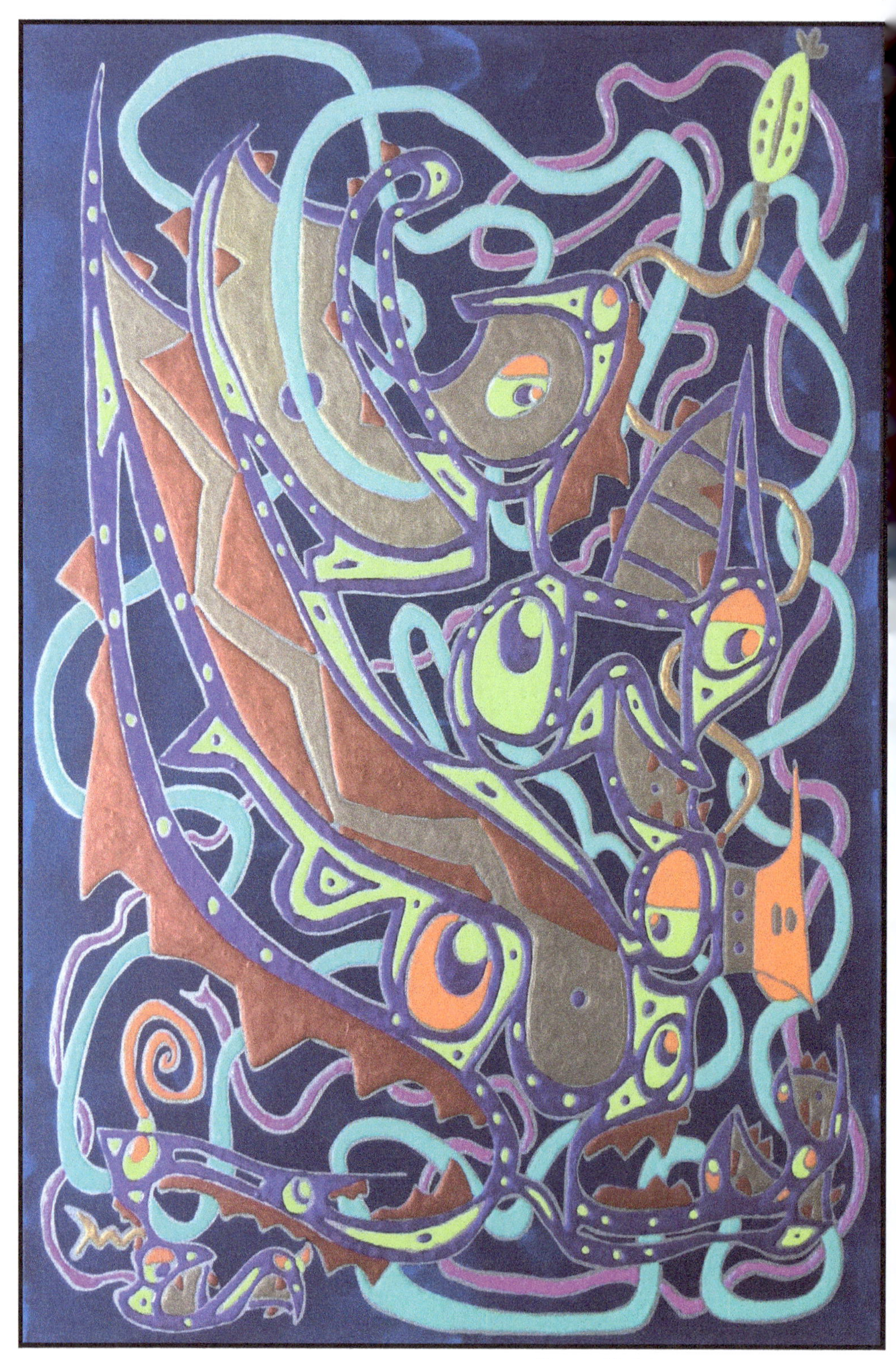

Tongue Twister

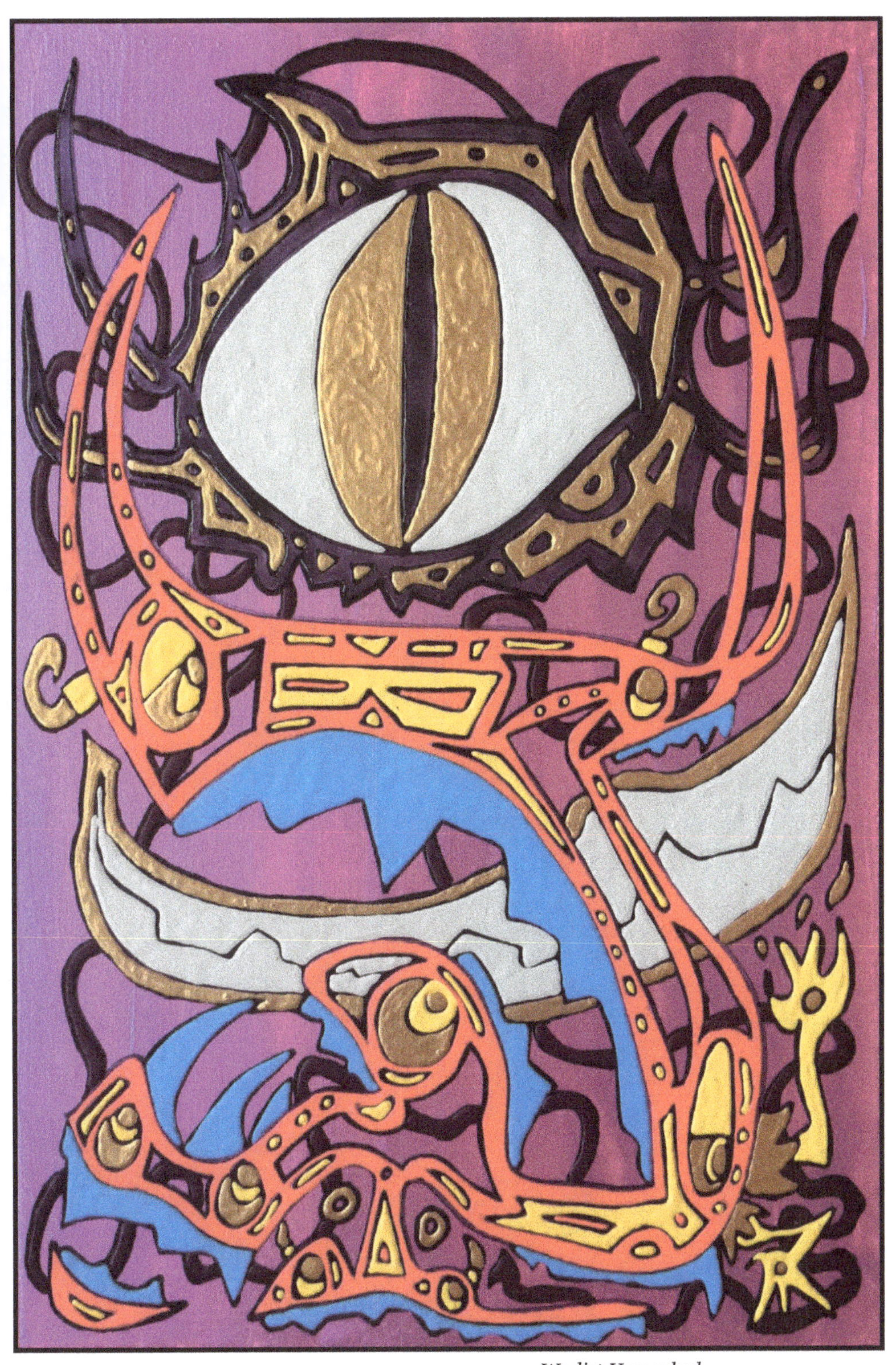

Wadjet Unmasked

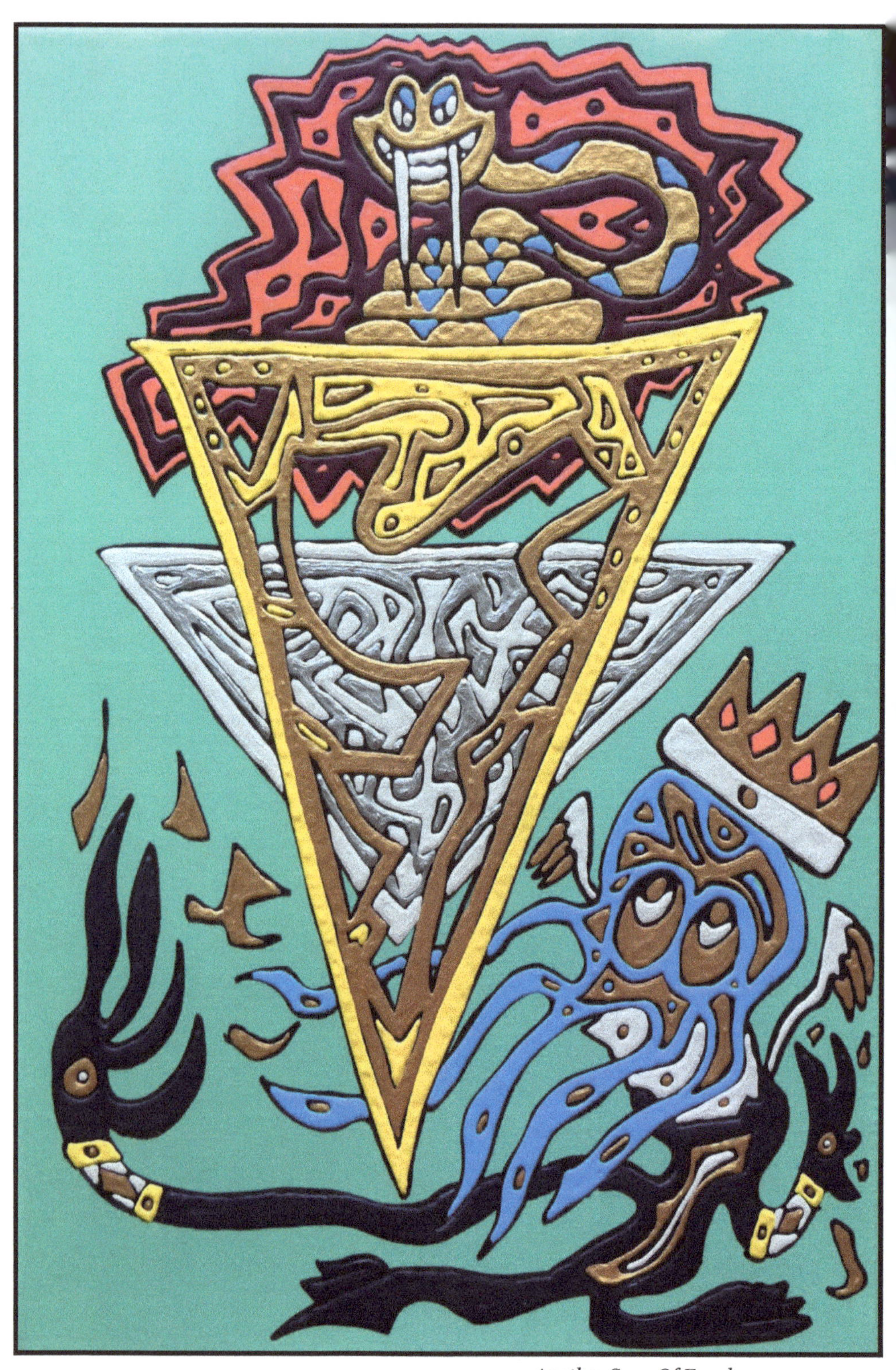

Another Song Of Freedom

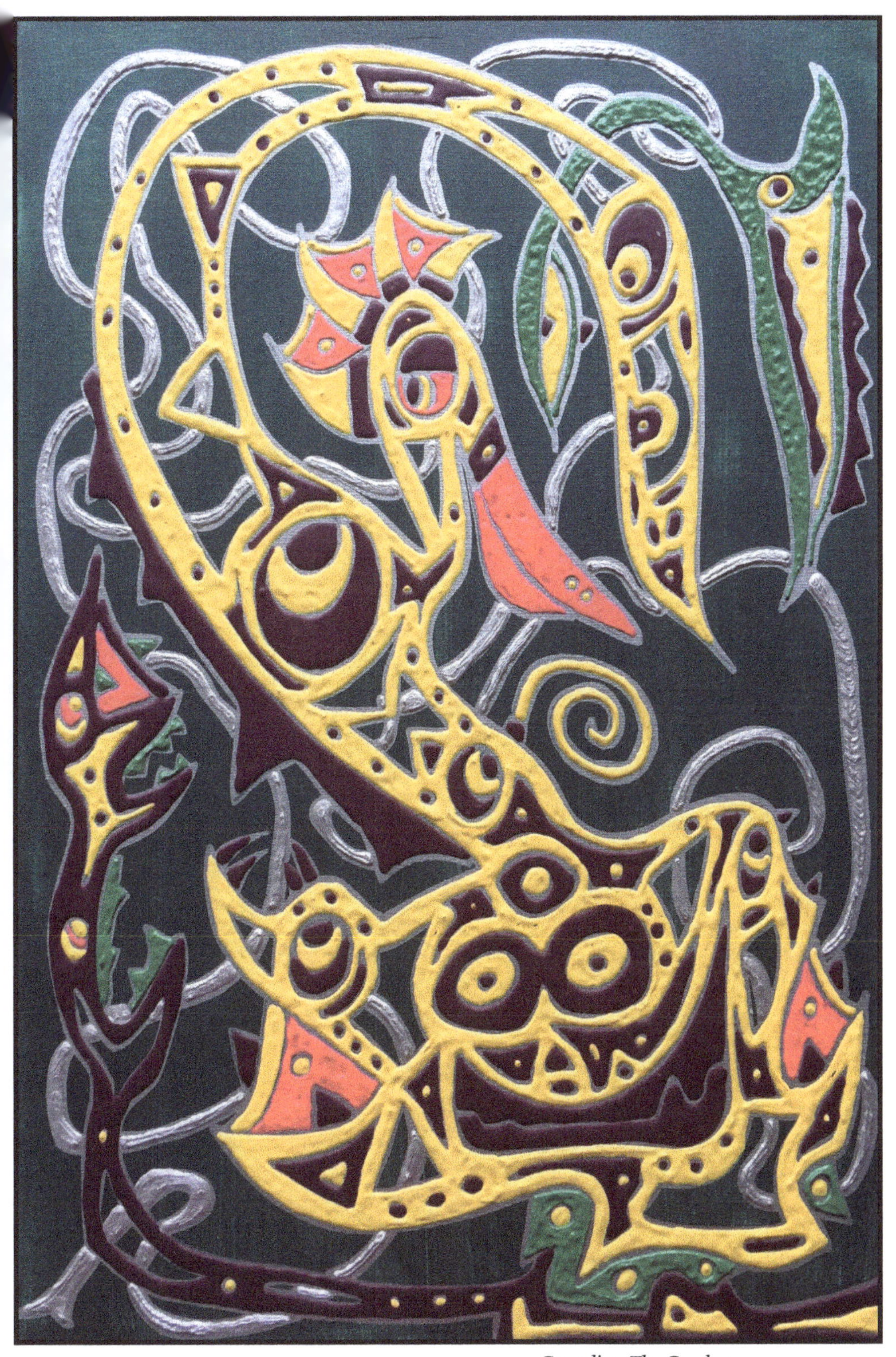

Guarding The Garden

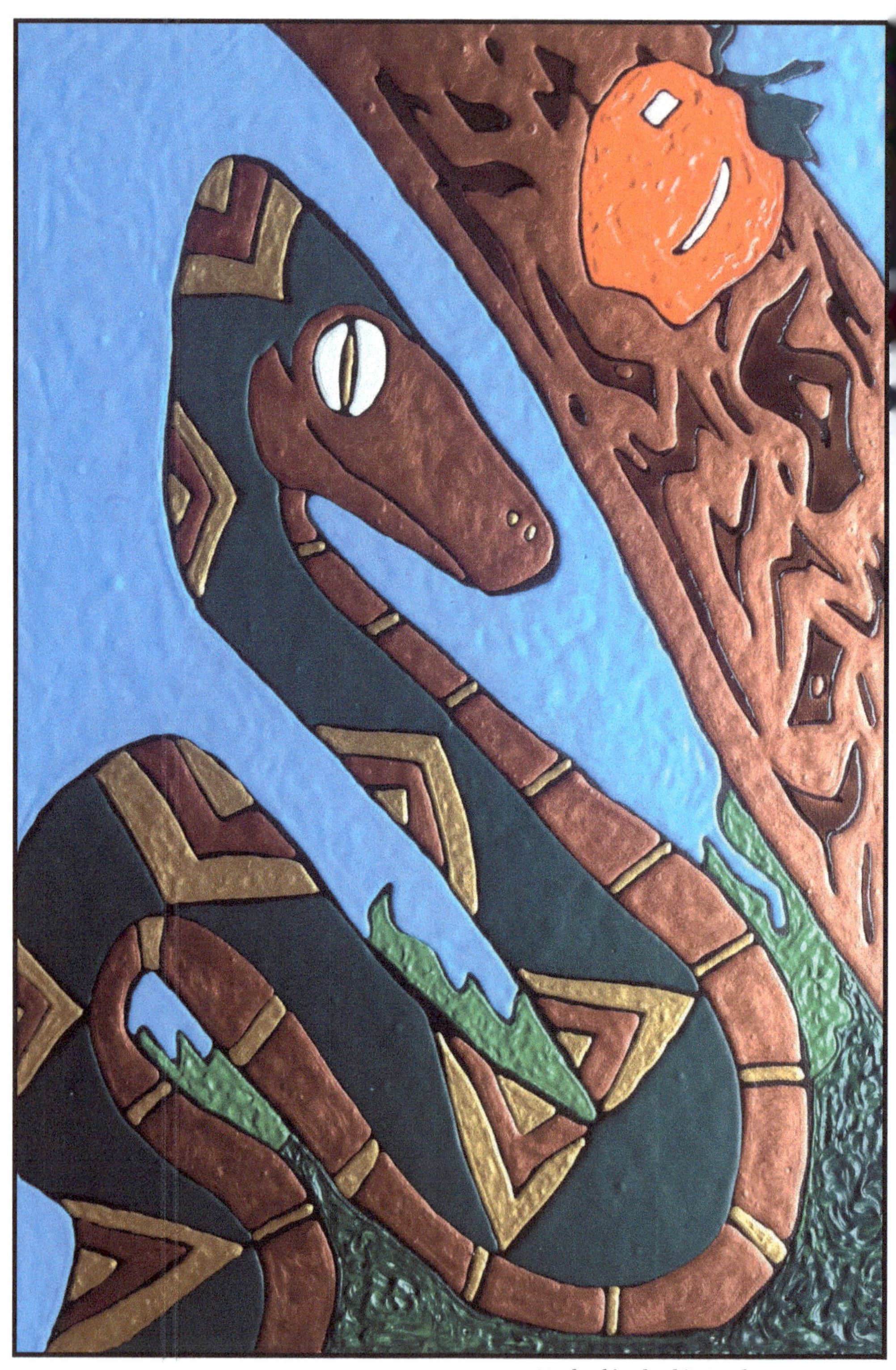

Nachash's Akashic Catch 22

Christians from Outer Space

Gregg Sapp

Did the Mangod, Jesus, only visit
this bluish and rock-strewn planet alone?
Was His life, symbolic or explicit,
exclusive to these mortals and their own?
'Tis vain to presume that we primates,
homo sapiens, here on this third orb,
were solely entrusted with transcendent fates,
the divine truth ours alone to absorb.
Imagine, then, that of myriad Earths,
ours hosted just an instant of His grace,
where despite the Christ's immaculate birth
He was treated ill by our fickle race.
Step under the starry dome of our sky
and ponder Saviors at each point on high.

In Virgo, there's a terrestrial globe
Where the Kabballax profess deference
to a God virgin-spawned by divine probe,
perfect from any frame of reference.
There, the Incarnate was duly installed
by rite of proboscis circumcision,
leader of the Council, its members called
to spread an ecumenical vision,
espoused through prophecies and miracles
persuasive enough to arrest all doubt,
proving true faith through valid oracles
and peace that no creature need live without.
Thus, this deity duly presided
over a world where goodwill resided.

Did the All-Loving Godhead then finish?
Nay, next She augured on a satellite
orbiting a gas giant in Canis,
where Her mission became a wretched plight.
Inhabited by Ologists, the minds
of this world dismissed Her revelation,
for prejudice and dogma always blinds
and base comfort is enough salvation.
So, upon bare, blistered and bleeding feet
She wandered alone across harsh terrain,

unheard, bent under the weight of defeat
only wind-driven dust to hear Her pain.
Another prophet with no following,
pursued only by her own shadowing.

Preach – through whatever open orifice,
in sonorous echoes or voiceless song,
snorts or sonar to the rapt populace,
by any means understood by the throng.
Pray – raising clenched fists, in brow-twisting thought,
while babbling glossolaliac nonsense
that belief dictates must be so if sought
by invoking a god in present tense.
Profess – declare faith, bear eager witness
to revealed doctrine or such sure dogma
told by priest, soothsayer, or pythoness
bearing soul-to-flesh soldered stigmata.
What's sensed by spirit becomes ritual
when reduced to memes and made scriptural.

Whither next will the Omniscient traverse
to inspire more novel epiphanies?
Whether mocked and abused, or praised in verse,
each virgin birth brings hopes and infamies.
Perchance the transcendent wandering Word
shall sojourn with Dharma in Orion,
whose cults expect an amiable Lord
smiling behind the aqua horizon.
So, somewhere, an improved Christ may appear,
for better aliens with free will to choose
whether It reveals a truth to revere,
or spews blasphemy to scorn and refuse.
Any god can be lauded or denied,
and thus adored, ignored, or crucified.

Amen.

The Works of Silas Plum

Silas Plum

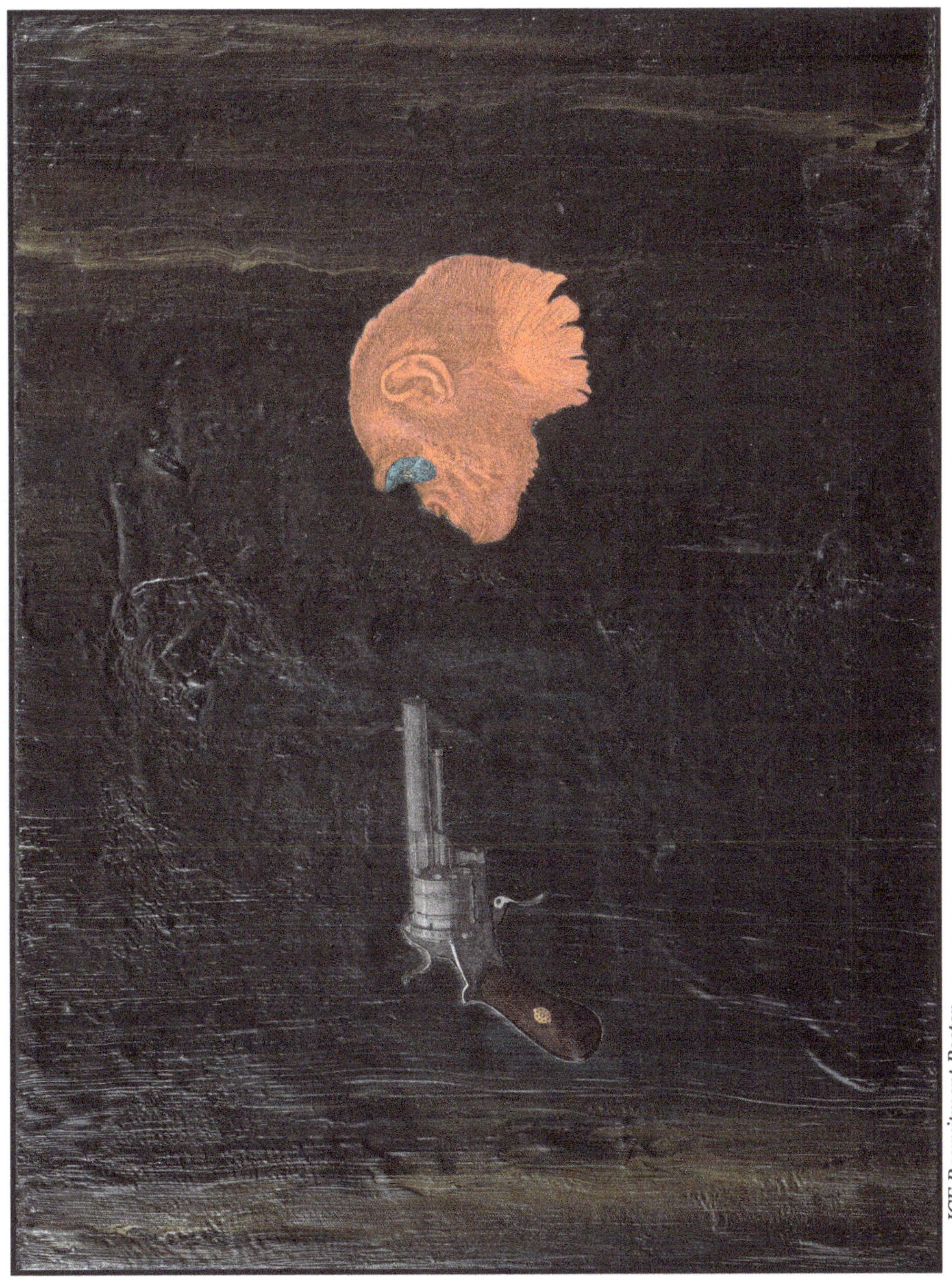

ICE Recruitment Poster

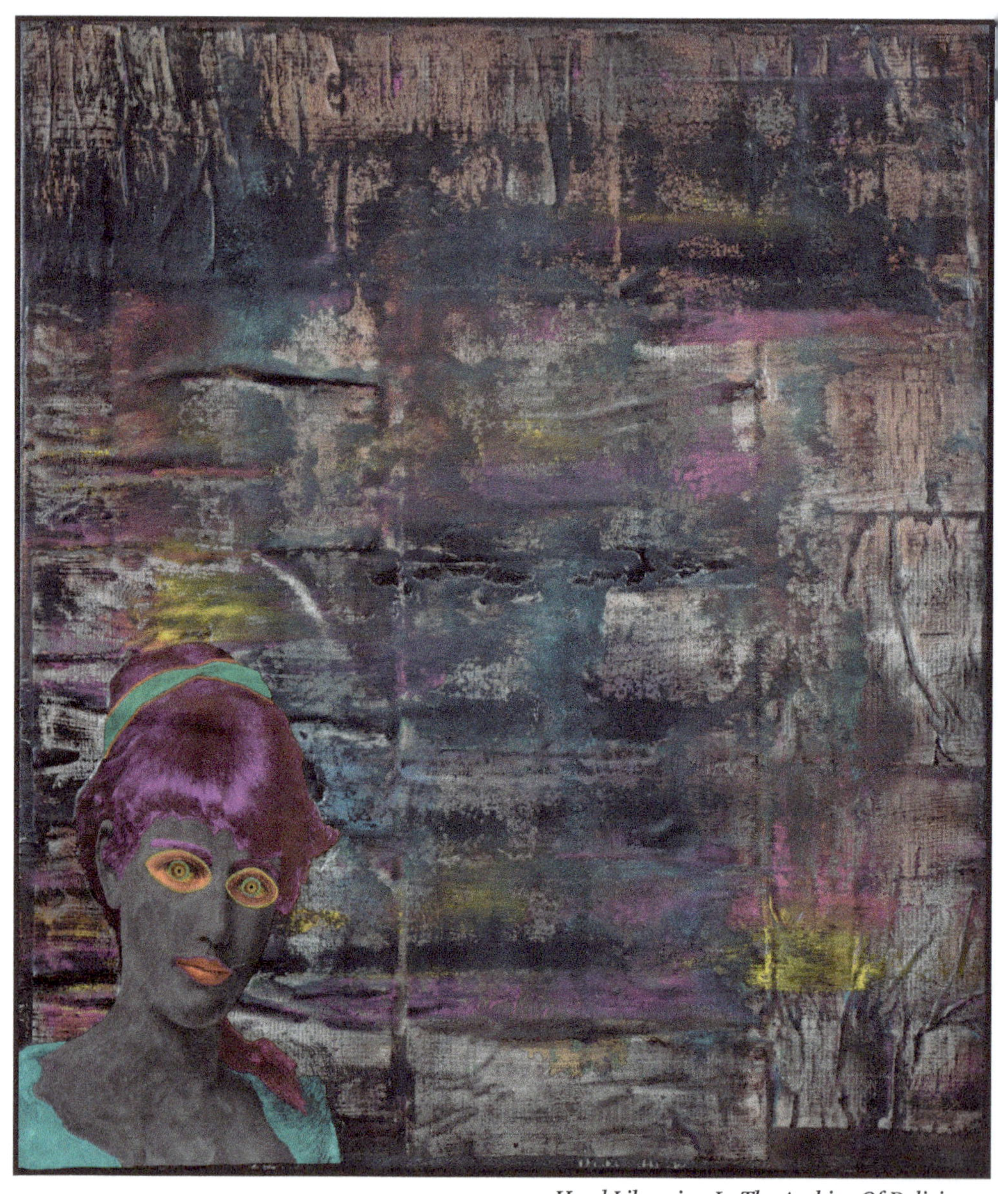

Head Librarian In The Archive Of Delirium

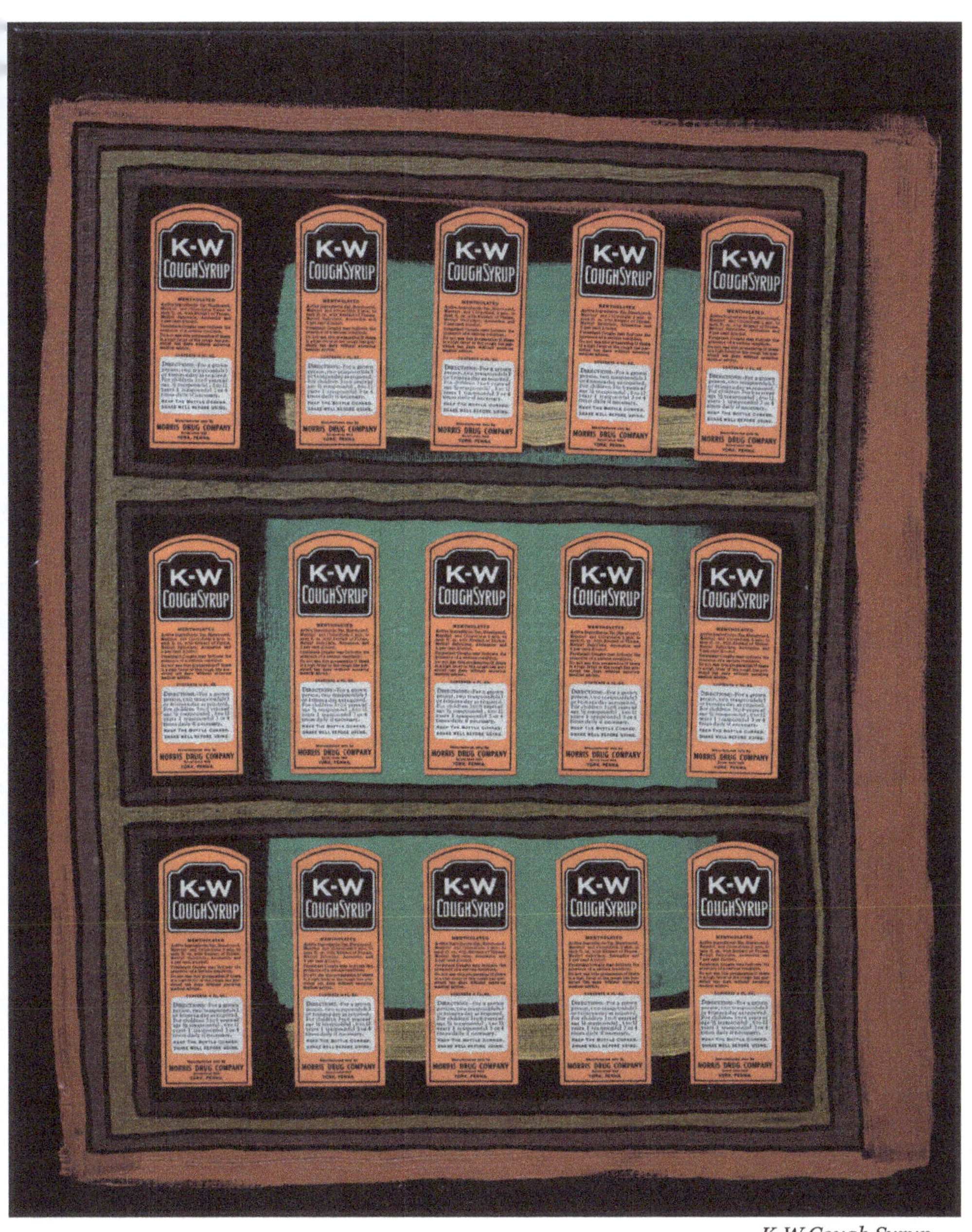

K-W Cough Syrup

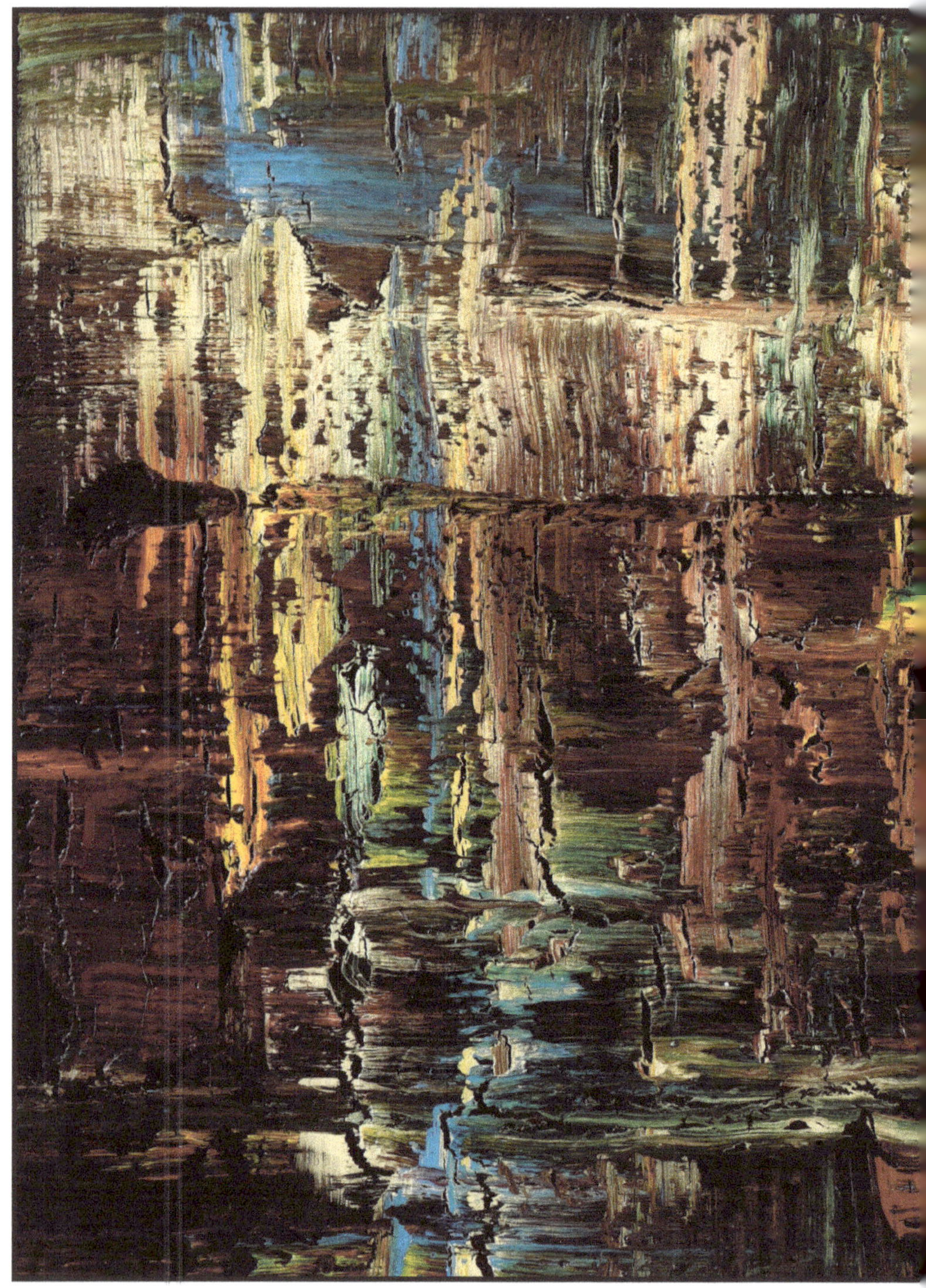

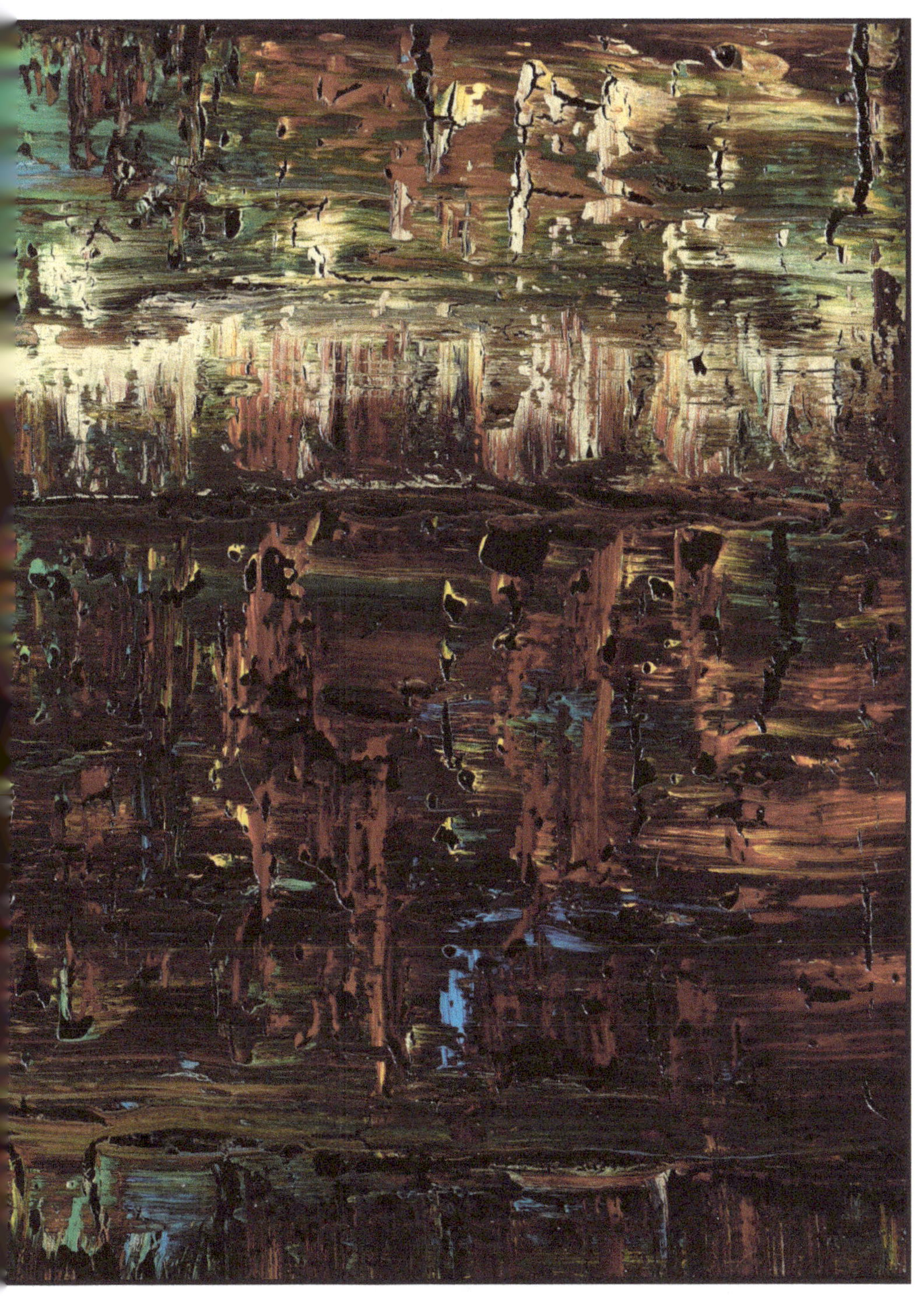

Canyon Reflected in Lake

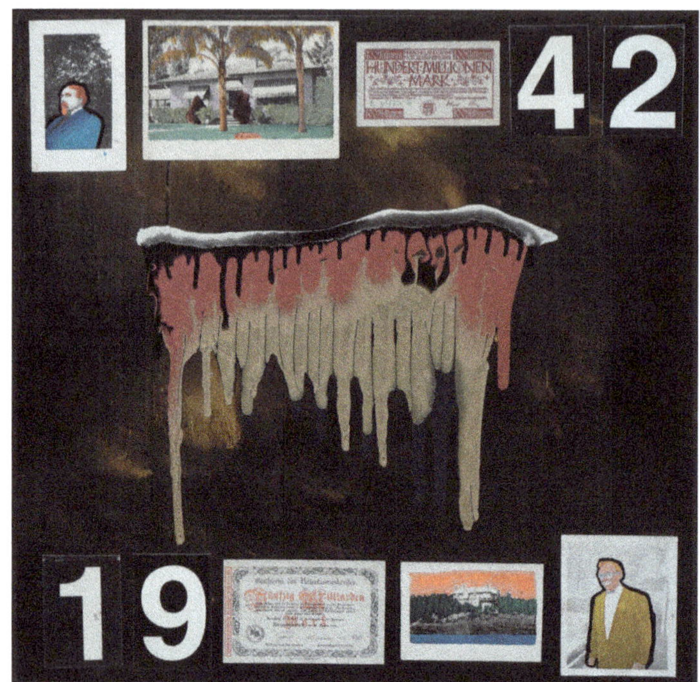

Florida 1942

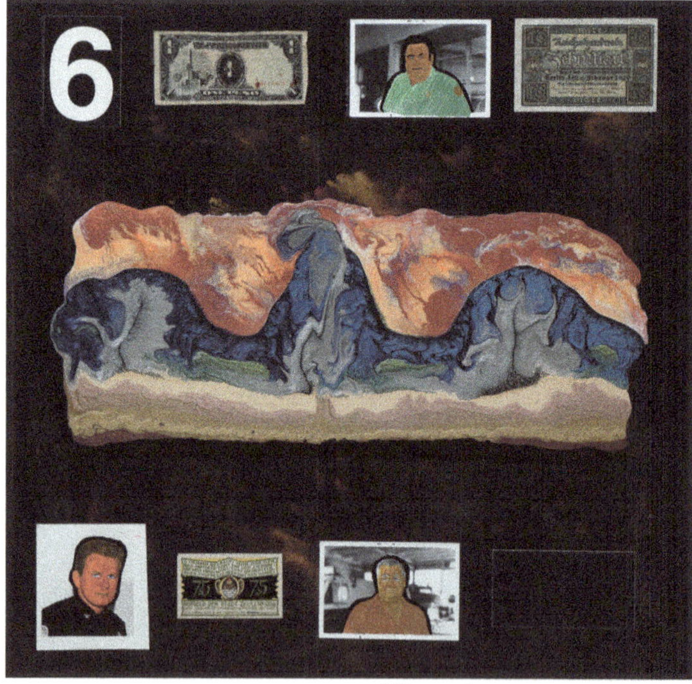

Ohio 1976

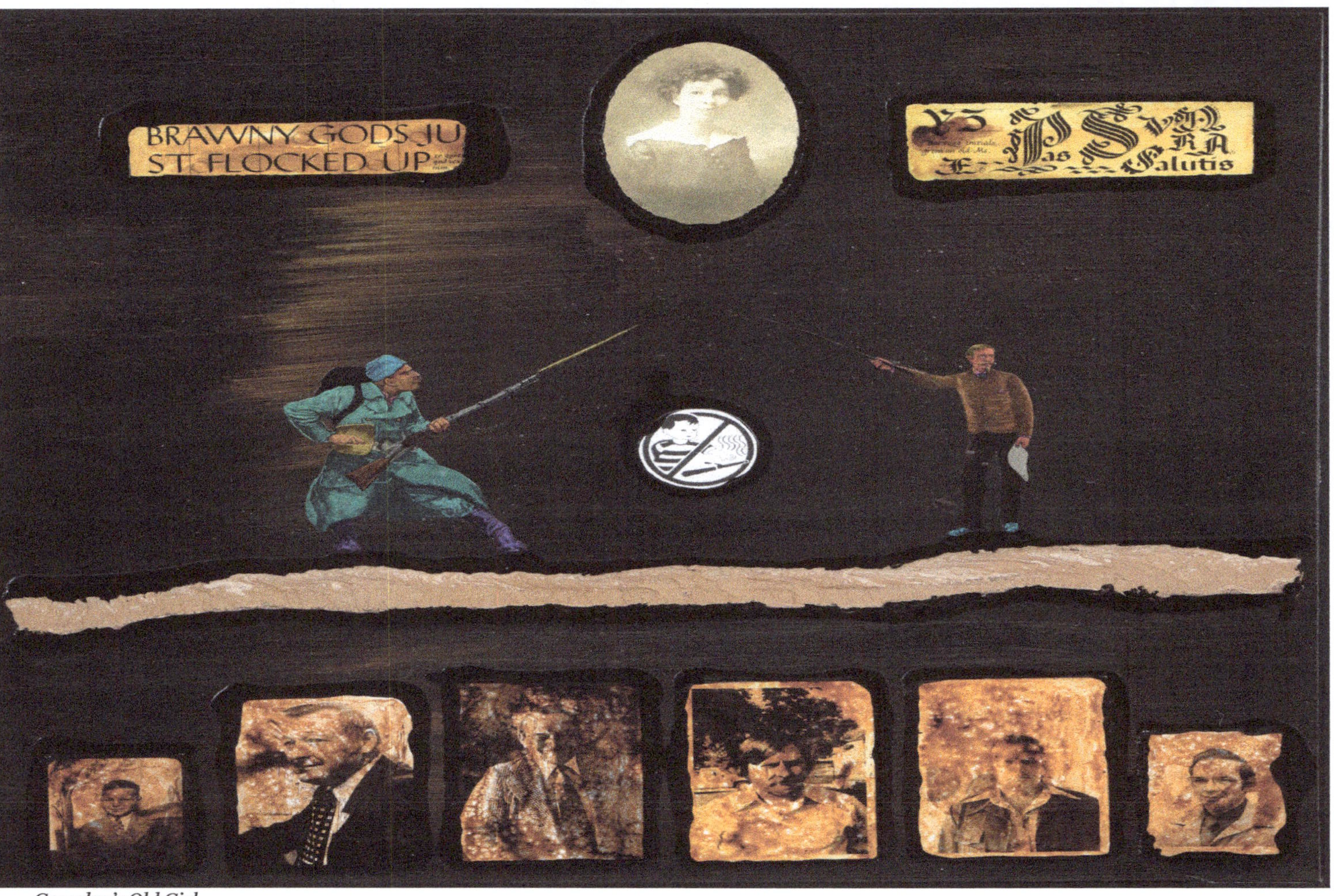

Grandpa's Old Girl

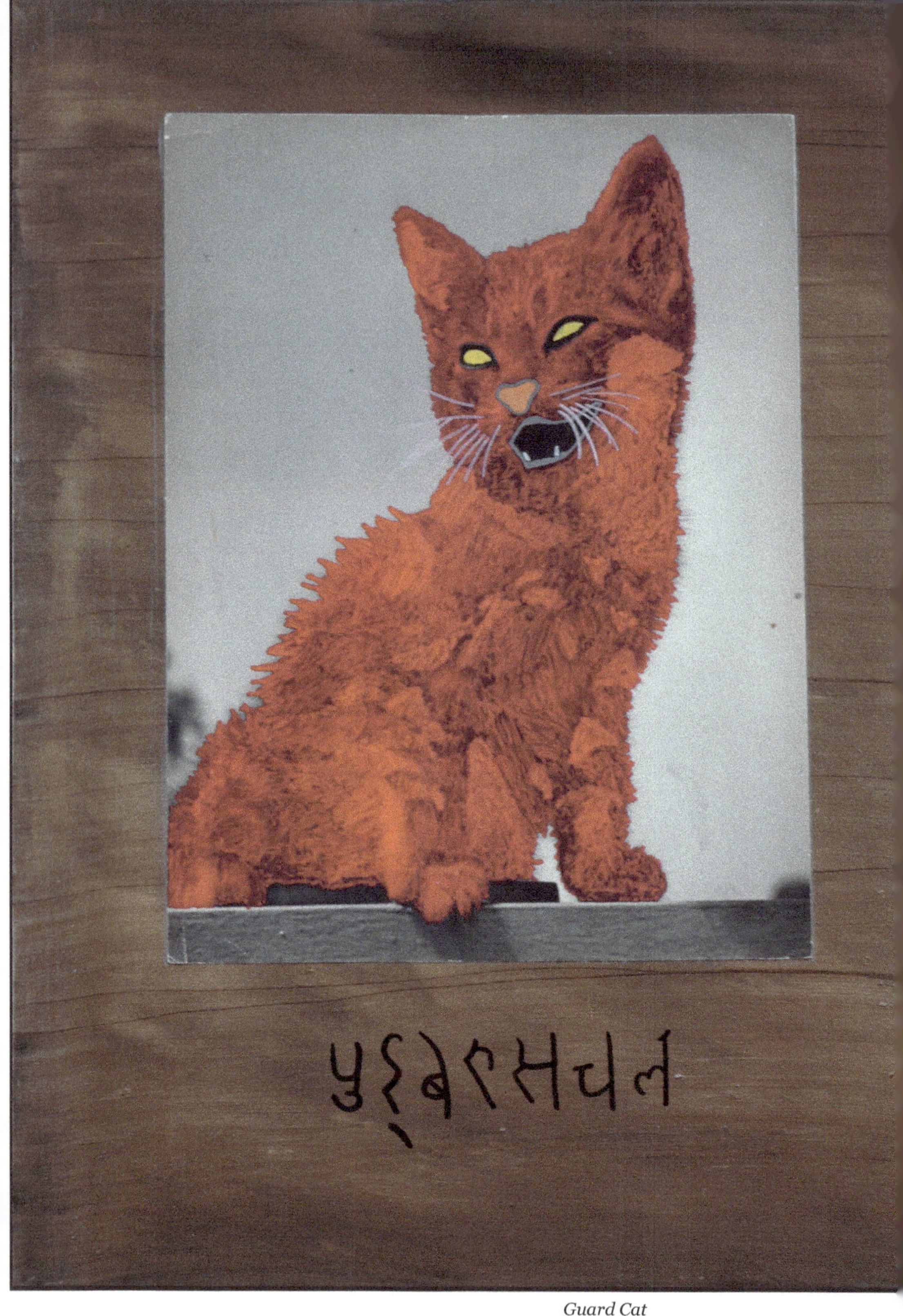

Guard Cat

Thirteen Ways of Looking at a Cat

Sebastian Correa

I

The stealthy feline
rises onto the table
and sits in
defiance.

II

Among the exceptional beasts,
the only one that thinks
like a human
is a cat.

III

Purring soft as
katydid wings—
I fall asleep to
a cats ruminations.

IV

The age-old question:
to love the servile sycophant of a dog?
Or the freethinking paws
of a cat?

V

Silky slits for eye.
impatient, cunning—
fangs of power—
the cat dominates,
and I submit.

We all submit.

VI

Dogs have pulled sleds,
hunted and done
our dirty work, deeds:
to toil and sweat and die!
Cats have
been god and goddesses,
infallible ferocious felines—
free.

VII

I love a cat
because I love rebellion

VIII

Somewhere
an ecosystem is thriving.
The outdoor cat must be
slaughtering to change this fact

IX

A cat
and independence
are one.
A cat and a lion and a tiger
are one.
A cat and a lion and a tiger
and independence
are one.

X

Unfettered by rules
of mere mortals
a cat plays
with its prey.

XI

Bastest trumps Anubis
Bastet so beautiful!
Full breasts and knowledge—
A cat is more a masterpiece
than the pyramids of Giza

XII

The corpulent kitty
crashed
on the couch
its
capricious, captious claws,
alien eyes,
bewitching heart
decide
if you are worthy of love .

XIII

The cat flicks its tail
and walks through the garden
into the opening
with a dead rodent in mouth,
which it drops near the front door—
it saunters back
into the forest.

We Are Hot Boyz™: Seven Memos

Michael Stigman

1.   WELCOME MEMO

Welcome to the new Hot Boyz™ touring season! Each of you, including newest member Lance (a memo on Lance soon!), has read and given thumbs up to the terms of employment. Here's a condensed version (a lot less reading!) for you to post in a high-visibility spot on the Hot Boyz™ tour bus, maybe on the wall between PacMan and the full-length mirror. Check it out:

"Rules" for Members of Hot Boyz™

Preface to "Rules": The following "rules" are descriptive, not prescriptive, which means we don't have the attitude of My Way Or The Highway Boyz. But we know what works and, hey, these "rules" work. Years of marketing tests and hours of ogling teens in megamalls have given us a formula that will virtually guarantee success for Hot Boyz™ (which may be hereafter referred to as "The Franchise," "The Commodity," or maybe, in cheeky moments, "The Cool Machine").

Okay, let's get started:

RULE ONE: Be A Gentleman Hot Boy™

Each of you has tested positive for HETEROsexuality. Congratulations! Life as a Hot Boy™ will make you famous. With fame comes contact with teenage girls. Contact with teenage girls leads to relationships that might seem natural enough. Still, we would like to discourage you from these relationships. It will be better for Hot Boyz™, and if it's better for Hot Boyz™ it's better for you.

In the end though, we don't want to be toolios (read "parental"), so let us just say this: your famousness will complicate things, in part because you will be a media magnet. Interviewers will try to get you to dish details from your private life. Listen up: If and when the Have You Two Done It question is asked, you are required to answer in the following manner: "We love each other very much but we are going to wait until we're married to perform the nasty." Memorize this statement and practice grilling each other with versions of the question and the Hot Boyz™ sanctioned answer. In regard to the nasty, in no case is a Hot Boy™ to engage in it, although great pains should be taken by each Hot Boy™ to make the fan base wonder what you would be like to cuddle with afterward.

RULE TWO: Facial-Hair-A-No-Go

Facial hair is generally prohibited, and not because it's creepy. Sometimes it's not. We'll be the judge. However, facial hair suggests a chummy familiarity with puberty, which is not what Hot Boyz™ is about. Hot Boyz™ is about chill, rockin' music that doesn't mean any harm. Puberty, on the other hand, has caused a lot of harm (e.g., unwanted pregnancies, acne).

Now, remember the thing about "We'll be the judge"? If you wish to modify your look by sporting facial hair, you must nominate yourself at Who's Ready For A Makeover? decision meetings, which occur one week prior to the album photo shoot. In rare cases where we do decide to allow facial hair, no two members of Hot Boyz™ will ever sport facial hair at the same time. That is creepy. Hot Boyz™ is not Lynrd Skynrd™.

In any event, even if we choose you as Who's Ready For A Makeover? and so permit the introduction of facial hair to your face, you will not actually grow facial hair. Instead, you will be permitted to present the appearance of high-maintenance facial hair, for which you will need to see Debby in makeup (she used to work for Prince). She will hook you up.

RULE THREE, PART A: Act Your Hot Boyz™ Age

Hot Boyz™ say things like, "Are you gonna hit the shaved ice stand tonight? It should be killer." In short, Keep It Light (KIL), unless we've told you to Go Introspective (GI). And in the case of GI, Hot Boyz™ should wonder aloud who invented hate. But don't be a downer: within five minutes of a GI statement, follow with a KIL statement: "Y'all Want This Party Started, Right?" Also, the word "like" is a Hot Boy'z best friend, as in "I, like, really like that reality TV show. Like a lot." By contrast, Hot Boyz™ never mention interest rates, racial profiling, or say things like, "A party? But they're calling for a 40% chance of precipitation." Yuck, Hot Boyz™!

RULE THREE, PART B: Down With Hot Boyz™ Interests

Hot Boyz™ show no detectable interest in activities that suggest maturity or adulthood. Instead, Hot Boyz™ profess a love for text messaging, video

video games (non-violent ones only), hanging out, and running across the front yard in the middle of a downpour yelling, "Life is crazy and so am I!" Also, in moments of vulnerability, Hot Boyz™ admit to having never had the heart to throw out their old collection of stuffed animals.

The key here: connect to the fan base, never giving them the opportunity to wonder, "Isn't he a bit too old for me?" You are, or will be if your career as a Hot Boy™ rocks, but that's beside the point. Not only your fans, but your fans' parents should never see you as the sort of teenager who has "older ideas," if you get our meaning. If not, then here: "Older ideas" are the sort that get their daughters in trouble on dates (again, as in "unwanted pregnancies"). As a Hot Boy™, you are incapable of that sort.

Okay, that's it for now. Keep your eyes peeled for additional memos. Peace out!

2. WELCOME LANCE MEMO

Let's welcome Lance, the newest Hot Boy™ to join us! Lance replaces Chris, who let us just say, did not behave as a Hot Boy™ should and, in other words, never really was Hot Boy™ material. (Seriously, was it only us, or did something just not add up with him?). Anyway, although Chris had been Caucasian-in-Dreadlocks™ Hot Boy™ and Lance is his replacement, we made a command decision that instead of simply making Lance the Caucasian-in-Dreadlocks™ Hot Boy™, we would take this opportunity to introduce a new Hot Boy™ type, one we've been dying to show.

Lance, then, is (drumroll please) Smoldering Garage Mechanic™ Hot Boy™, which basically means he's really hot *and* good with his hands. You just know that if an amplifier blew on stage, Lance could rip it apart in no time and get it working again. Same for the tour bus. Another thing: smoldering means he doesn't say much, which means, for you other Hot Boyz™, press conferences are "not really his thing" and you'll have to take up the slack. Beyond this, we're not going to oversteer this new type. As we go, we'll work the ins and outs of what else Smoldering Garage Mechanic™ Hot Boy™ means. Stay posted. In the meantime, let's give a Hot Boyz™ welcome to Lance!

3. JUST TO GET SOME THINGS STRAIGHT MEMO, Or More Like Here's A Clarification Of Who We Are: Authorial Intention, Or Explaining Song Lyrics

Since last week's posting of the basic "rules" of Hot Boyz™ behavior, we are happy to report that the "rules" have already begun to produce this season's seeds of success for Hot Boyz™! We don't want to go into too much detail yet, but we'll give you a hint: stay out of the sun in order to have a video-friendly complexion (!).

Despite this note of success (pun intended), in order to maintain forward progress for The Franchise, we feel it necessary to clarify some points of what Hot Boyz™ is all about. Being a member of Hot Boyz™ means you are a Voice in Society that says, "We know the world is full of pain and ugliness, but we're not here to make you feel uncomfortable about it, let alone responsible for it. Even for our occasional songs about hot social issues we lay down rock-steady beats, and you can satisfy your activist-urge by tapping your foot to the rhythm. And in case you're wondering, we know you don't have time to protest wars in Iraqistan or whatever it is. Neither do we." We say "Support the President," which is to say Hot Boyz™ are Non-Political in all they do and say, and how they move on stage and in (future) videos.

That's why, in the spirit of true Hot Boyz™ spirit, we write and produce songs like, "Choose Your Path (baby)." Now, if one of you wants to criticize, in the privacy of the Hot Boyz™ dressing room, the artistic value of any Hot Boyz™ song—let's take this one for example—you need to know that "Choose Your Path (baby)" is not a "bullshit, nonsense, inane" song, as somebody put it. Think about the lines, "When you come to the fork in the road, take it!" which is anything but nonsense or inane, let alone bullshit. It's about making decisions, it's a nod to an American poet for godsakes, and it means if you look deep enough you'll see the hidden meaning.

4. UNPRECEDENTED ACTION MEMO: An Additional "Rule," As Made Necessary By A Certain Situation That Has Come To Our Attention

The Franchise's regard for artistic expression by members of The Franchise extends to but is limited by members' artistic expressions of sanctioned, scripted, and rehearsed expressions. We write the songs. We know what they mean. Any unintended interpretation is simply wrong. To give an example of what we're talking about here: If in concert the song being sung has the lines: "I've been crying so much/like buckets of rainwater/

that sit until algae forms/to make greenish water," take it from us, mister, crying is an appropriate accompaniment to the singing. More to the point, we do not recognize and have no patience for expressions of ironic intent by members of Hot Boyz™. You Know Who You Are, and the three-piece algae suit was not funny. And guess what? Wardrobe is sending you the bill.

5. ADDENDUM TO THE RULES FOR HOT BOYZ™ MEMO: That Thingy In The Preface

Preface: In the original preface to the original rules, there was that thing about how we didn't want to go my way or the highway. Bump that shit. Due to some, albeit age-appropriate, authority-testing/baby bird spreading his wings and trying to fly/too-big-for-britches behavior/etc., for the sake of Hot Boyz™ pecuniary interests and solvency, we have to hereby lay down the law.

NEW RULE: Appropriate Live-Stage Behavior

Members of Hot Boyz™, when in live concert, are always encouraged to kneel when singing ballads, to lean close enough to fans to allow for the grasping and tearing of clothes (if wearing tear-proof Hot Boyz™ leather pants), and to accept bouquets of roses, friendship bracelets, Beanie Babies™, etc. from fans. Any banter with the audience should be limited to audience flattery, with statements like, "We're so glad to be back in <u>Current City</u>," or "<u>Current City</u>, You Rawk!"

Hot Boyz™ are never permitted to ad lib. Here's what we don't like. The song is, "Reach For Your Goal, Squeeze It, Seize It" right? And someone decides to introduce it with a story about a serial killer who did hand-strengthening exercises in order to better strangle his victims. What can we say? We didn't think we had to make a rule against this one. I'm not going to name names, but your initials are Lance. Do it again and you might find yourself with worse problems than a headset microphone that has somehow stopped working.

6. NEW RULE FOR PRESS CONFERENCES MEMO: Never Thought We'd Have To Make A Rule Against This One, Either

We have dress rehearsals for Hot Boyz™ Going On Tour and Hot Boyz™ Have A New Album press conferences so that we can prepare you for the sort of questions members of the music press may ask. If you remember our asking you in rehearsals to describe your lifelong dream, an appropriate response, if you remember, is Fusion. As in, "I have always wanted to fuse together my love of Rap and Pop." The appropriate response is not, "I don't know about lifelong, but I keep having this dream starring Gwen Stefani and a lot of popsicles."

7. RECONNAISANCE MEMO: Are You Still With Me, Hot Boyz™?

We could beat ourselves up about this one from now till kingdom come, but what good would it do? We could second-guess ourselves. Now that we think about it, we can see that while Caucasian-in-Dreadlocks would tend to mellow out Hot Boyz™, as it turns out, Garage Mechanic Hot Boyz™ would more likely smolder until pent-up teen angst turns a freestyle rap into a maniacal rant. We only wish he hadn't decided to say such hurtful things about Sexy Athlete™ Hot Boy™ and David Lee Roth™ Hot Boy™.

Now, Who's Ready For A Makeover?

cronos devoured his children

Art by Jada Fabrizio
Poetry by J. Summerisle Wilson

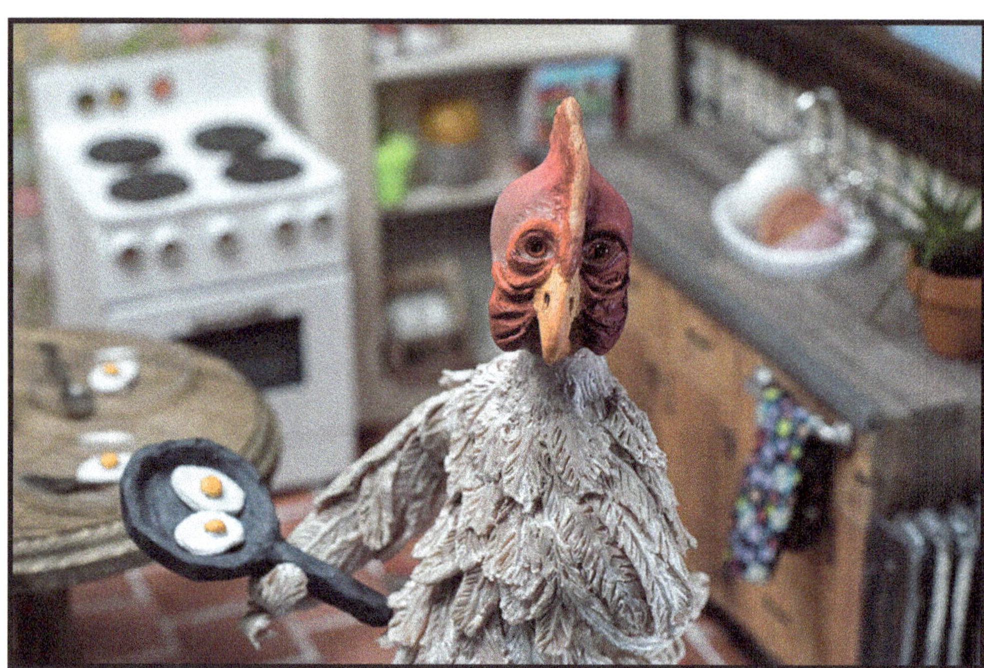

and now we come
confused. the dawn
is hungry and we
cannot relinquish
our dreams.

       O take
our reason with hardness,
make us soft as eggs.
don't ask us
       what came first?
or   who are we?

our stomachs outstrip
sleep & reach deep
for the ugly things
inside of us.

call it hunger,
hot beyond this grief
that gnarls & nibbles.
let us fix our horror
for a feast before
we realise, before
the truth rises in
mourning to make us
who really we are.

In Order Of Appearance:

Thomas Boos recently graduated from the University of Pittsburgh with a degree in creative writing. He is applying for MFA programs, and submitting work for publication.

Caitlin Jackson is a graduate of Oberlin College, where she received a BA in Creative Writing and German Studies. She also completed her MFA in Creative Writing at the University of Central Florida. She has had poems published in 2river View, Natural Bridge, The Jabberwock Review, OVS, Grey Sparrow Journal and Scissors and Spackle. Her short story, "Swell", was published in Painted Bride Quarterly. Her first full length poetry collection, Myths for Small Matters, was published in December 2016 by Main Street Rag Publishing.

Meimei Xu is a senior at the Westminster Schools in Atlanta, GA. She is a recipient of two National Gold Medals for journalism from the Alliance for Young Artists and Writers and a Gold Key recipient for poetry and memoir. Her writing has been recognized by the Library of Congress and the NCTE Superior Writing Achievement Award, and her work has been published in Typishly. She currently works as a content writer for The Adroit Journal.

Emily Somoskey is a visual artist and educator from Akron, OH. She attended The University of Akron's Mary Schiller Myers School of Art, in Akron, OH and received a BA in Art Education with a minor in painting in 2013. She is currently a 2nd year MFA candidate at Michigan State University, located in East Lansing, MI. Emily's current work explores the ways we interface with material culture in our everyday lives, specifically the relationships formed between objects and individuals within the constructed domestic living space.

Elliot C. Mason is a PhD candidate at Queen Mary, University of London, researching whiteness and race theory in contemporary British poetry. His poems have been published in various media, including Exclamat!on, Undercurrent Philosophy, De Sur a Sur, [smiths] and the We Will Be Free anthology, as well as displayed at the Migration Museum. He is the winner of both the University of Bolton Poetry Competition and the Bart Moore-Gilbert Essay Prize 2018. He is also a playwright, and his political comedies have been on at many London theatres, the latest of which – 'Everything Today is the Same' – will reopen at the Camden Fringe Festival in August 2019. He has translated the poetry of A. K. Blakemore, Rachael Allen and Sara Torres between English/Spanish.

Monica Stevens-Kirby is a writer and artist from Georgia, where she practices psychotherapy and teaches at the University level. Her writing is published in various literary presses and academic journals. Monica finds combining images and words appealing. The notion of poems as paintings and vice versa tend to be her most thoughtful works.

Haley Karin is an intersectional feminist, poet, and proposal writer for a non-profit organization in Northern California, where she lives with her boyfriend and their kitten Cosmo. She earned her B.A in English from California State University, Sacramento in 2015 and her poems have been published by The Tule Review, 805 Lit + Art, Burrow Press, and The Sacramento Voices Anthology. In 2017 her piece "Cover Girl" was selected as a finalist for the Fortnight Prize by Eyewear Publishing Ltd. In 2018 her poetry was nominated for Best of the Net and The 2020 Pushcart Prize. You can follow her social media handle @poetrybyhaley to keep up with her latest news.

Based in New York City, artist Mizuki Nishiyama works with acrylics to create raw, vivid, and multi-layered paintings.The raw human passion is the overarching theme of her work. Nishiyama's paintings strive to explore the nature of vulnerability, the extreme, and human fragility.

Nancy worked as a writer, performer and collaborator in experimental theatre in NYC. for twelve years. The highlights include; The Wooster Group, internationally touring her own monologues, and her devised group collaborations for the International Theatre Festival in London. She worked as a Senior Lecturer in contemporary Theatre and Performance in Manchester, England. Nancy has published numerous academic essays and short fictions. Her performance work is cited in, Savran, David,(1986) Breaking the Rules, TCG Inc., N,Y., N.Y. and Guerrilla Performance and Multimedia, (2001), Editors Hill L., Paris H., Continuum Books, N.Y.& London. Some examples of her publications are: Reilly-McVittie, N.O. (1989), "A Black Dress Decision", Bateria Magazine for the Arts, Germany, (Editor: Bush, W), Nuremberg Press, Nuremberg. Reilly-McVittie, N.O. (1990), "Last Night a DJ Saved my Life, between C & D", Journal for the Arts, Editor, Joel Rose, Independent Press, Summer, (Editor: Rose, J), Independent Press. Reilly-McVittie, N.O. (2005), "A Realism Runs Through It: How Liz LeCompte and the Wooster Group Remediated Realism in 'Route One and Nine'", American Mirrors (Self) Reflections and (Self) Distortions, (Editor: Lopez Liquete, M), University of the Basque Country Press Service, Spain, pp 261-267. Nancy has returned to the use of her single name.

Meggan Joy is a self-taught photographic artist primarily focused on digital collage. Joy combines fragments of the natural sciences with her narratives and allegories; often weaving in symbols and motifs from art history to create a new surreal vision. She fabricates this staged imagery from the ground up, growing most of her subject matter in her garden, documenting the growth, beauty and decay. Each piece is created by assembling thousands of individual photographs of botanicals, insects and other wildlife - resulting in a final image that is bursting with life and layered with hidden details and anecdotes.

Patrick T. Reardon is the author of eight books, including the poetry collection Requiem for David and Faith Stripped to Its Essence, a literary-religious analysis of Shusaku Endo's novel Silence. His poetry has appeared in Silver Birch Press, Cold Noon, Eclectica, Esthetic Apostle, Ground Fresh Thursday, Literary Orphans, Rhino, Spank the Carp, Main Street Rag, Down in the Dirt, Time for Singing, Tipton Poetry Journal, Under a Warm Green Linden and The Write City, and he has been nominated for a Pushcart Prize twice. Reardon, who worked as a Chicago Tribune reporter for 32 years, has published essays and book reviews widely in such publications as the Tribune, Chicago Sun-Times, Crain's Chicago Business, National Catholic Reporter and U.S. Catholic. His novella Babe was short-listed by Stewart O'Nan for the annual Faulkner-Wisdom Contest. His Pump Don't Work blog can be found at http://www.patricktreardon.com/blog/.

Eimear Bourke is an Irish idealist and perpetual dreamer. Raised in Navan, Co. Meath, she currently lives with her girlfriend in Dublin 6W. Driven by a belief in purpose and fatalism, her poems are shaped by themes such as nature, interpersonal relationships, sexuality and memory. She is inspired by Rita Ann Higgins and Yrsa Daley-Ward.

S Akhtar is a London based poet and playwright. They are interested in the intersection of madness and spirituality. They particularly focus on Abrahamic religions, psychosis and addiction.

Steven J. Wills is a writer and poet currently living in Medford, NJ. A graduate from The College of New Jersey, Mr. Wills holds an MA in English. Much of his work can be found on Instagram under the handle @copyrightsymbolsjw. He enjoys works of science-fiction and fantasy, outdoor activities, and making memories with friends and family.

Jenifer Fox is an author, educator, poet. A graduate of the Bread Loaf School of English, Jenifer's nonfiction titles published by Viking/Penguin and Jossey-Bass have won several awards. Her recent project is an ephraxis book with her partner oil painter, J. Chris Morel where Jenifer responded in poetry to 50 of Morel's landscape oil paintings. Their joint show, One Man's Home, One Woman's Heart opens at Nedra Matteucci Gallery in Santa Fe in June, 2019. Fox lives n Taos, NM. Her instagram handle is @jeniferfox.

Gregory studied art at FIT & SUNY Purchase in New York & Keene State in New Hampshire. In 1996, Gregory was one of ten FIT students selected to show in a group exhibit at OSilas Gallery in Yonkers, NY. Gregory has had 59 illustrations published in Surrender To The Flow Magazine and has illustrated the children's book TMWSIY (Based on the music of Phish, all proceeds donated to The Waterwheel Foundation). Scans of published works and book located on Gregory's website https://artfitzgerald.com

Gregg Sapp is a Pushcart Prize nominated writer, librarian, college teacher and academic administrator. He is the author of the "Holidazed" series of satirical novels, each of which is centered around a different holiday. The first two books, "Halloween from the Other Side" and "The Christmas Donut Revolution," will be published in 2019 by Evolved Publishing. His previous books include "Dollarapalooza" (Switchgrass Books, 2011) and "Fresh News Straight from Heaven," based upon the life and folklore of Johnny Appleseed (Evolved, 2018). He has published humor, poetry, and short stories in Defenestration, Waypoints, Semaphore, Kestrel, Zodiac Review, Marathon Review, and been a frequent contributor to Midwestern Gothic, and others. Gregg lives in Tumwater, WA.

At age 12, Silas Plum won the East Coast POG tournament. The prize was 500 POG's, small collectible cardboard circles, each with an identical red and blue design on the front. From that moment on, he became obsessed with the question of Value. Why were these important? How could anything not necessary for survival be worth more than anything that was? Does artistic sentiment have value? The POG's are gone, but the questions remain. Through assemblages of defunct currency, discarded photographs, and long-forgotten illustrations, Silas Plum challenges the idea of objective vs subjective value. He believes strongly in the tired old maxim that the true value of an object is more than the sum of its parts, that the gut is a truth-teller, and that the Aristotelian notion of learning-by-doing is the best teacher around. Judge his worth at silasplum.com.

Sebastian Correa is pursuing his MFA in Fiction at Southern Connecticut State University. Despite being a student of fiction, Sebastian loves to write poetry and songs and creations that exist within the intersection of prose and verse.

Michael Stigman grew up in Minnesota, has lived in both Virginia and Kansas, and now calls Missouri home, where he lives with his wife and children. He teaches creative writing and literature at a small college across the river in Kansas. He has published stories in Beloit Fiction Journal, Sycamore Review, South Dakota Review, Zone 3, and Suicidally Beautiful: A Collection of Sports Stories (Main Street Rag Press), among others.

Photographer Jada Fabrizio is passionately committed to story telling. She is an enthusiastic watcher of light and its effect it has on form. When she is not buliding sets in her studio or scuptling a creature for her photo stories she plays classical guitar and does freelance photography for medical institutions. Born in queens, New York, her formal education began at SUNY New Paltz. Where she studied creative writing and later photography at the School of Visual Arts And ICP (International Center of Photography) in New York City. Jada emphasizes the importance of capturing emotional experiences. "By not telling a complete story" she says, "It allows others to "feel" the photograph in their own way." She goes on to say, "I want the spectator to look at my photographs and experience their own reality through them."

J. Summerisle Wilson currently lives in the East Midlands of England & has appeared in various online journals. Her work has been nominated for Best of the Net 2020 and a full list of publications can be found at jenniferwilsonlit.wordpress.com. She may also be found on Twitter @_dead_swans

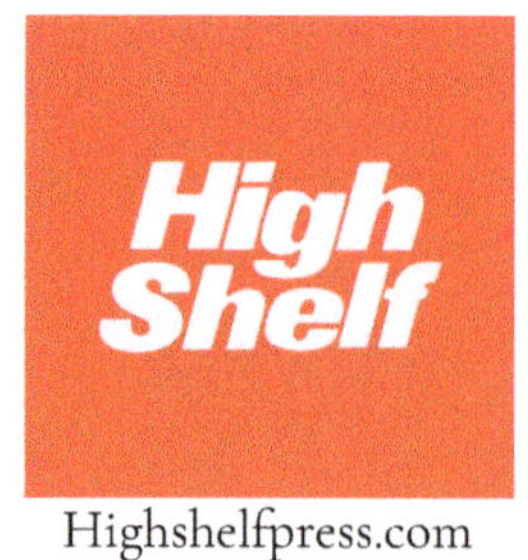

Highshelfpress.com

9 781733 027991